Catalyze Your Destiny!

Discover Who You Are, Reveal Your Purpose, and Launch Into Action

JORDAN RING

Disclaimer

Although the author and publisher have made every effort to ensure that the information in this book was correct at press time, the author does not assume and hereby disclaims any liability to any party for any loss, damage, or disruption caused by errors, or omissions, whether such errors or omissions result from negligence, accident, or any other cause.

Author further disclaims any liability for any party for the self-help advice and opinions on said subjects contained within this book. The information provided in this book is designed to provide helpful information on the subjects discussed. This book is not meant to be used, nor should it be used, to diagnose or treat any medical condition.

DEDICATION

I dedicate this book to two very dear friends. It's not every day that friends become family, and Tom and Cathy have substantially influenced the following words. It's not just the delicious coconut cakes Cathy whips up, nor is it solely Tom's enjoyable stories and positive attitude that prompt this dedication. It's so much more.

Their overwhelming support and availability, not only for my wife and me but also for countless other couples and individuals, is the reason I dedicate this book to them. I would not be where I am today without their encouragement, wisdom, and friendship. I am forever in their debt.

May this book forever be a part of their legacy.

FOREWORD

I'd like to start out this book by giving away the ending of another book. Tim Tebow (yes, the football player) recently wrote a children's book called *Bronco and Friends: A Party to Remember*.

In the story, a dog named Bronco is invited by his friends to a grand party. But you can't get in for free! To attend, you must bring a unique puzzle piece. Bronco helps his friends find their pieces along the way to the party. Once they arrive, Bronco turns to leave because he never found his own piece. However, the host appears and reveals that he has Bronco's piece. The host helps Bronco see that his purpose was to help everyone else find their puzzle piece and their way.

Why did I tell you this story? As you'll find out later in this book, it's not because Jordan is a huge fan of dogs (or cats). It's because Jordan has discovered (like Bronco) that his purpose in life is to help others discover what makes them unique and motivate them to relentlessly pursue their Destiny. How do I know this? Because he has done it for me.

Jordan is great at motivating others. What sets Jordan and this book apart is his expertise in helping others get organized and stay focused on achieving their dreams. I can tell when I haven't spent time with Jordan in a while. It's not that I stop dreaming. It's worse than that. I stop making progress toward the dream inside of me. As an ENFP on the Myers-Briggs Type Indicator, (which you'll learn more about in this book) I love chasing anything new. I also don't have one Executing theme in my Top 5 of CliftonStrengths. I need people like Jordan and books like this one to help me execute on my dreams.

As I have come to know Jordan over the years, he has blown me away by his strengths and wisdom. After reading this book, I realized Jordan did not just stumble upon his wisdom and passion to help others pursue their Destiny. He and his wife, Miranda, spent several years working in a variety of roles at retirement communities. As you probably know, spending time with the elderly can help you gain wisdom. They have had time to reflect on their lives, the good parts and the bad.

Based on what I have learned from Jordan's experience, there are too many people that look back on their lives with regret. I imagine you can only listen to so many of those stories before you know you don't want to make the same mistakes with your own life. I think those conversations served as motivational rocket fuel for Jordan and his purpose. Not only does Jordan not want to become someone that arrives at the end of his life to realize he didn't fulfill his Destiny, he doesn't want it for me or for you either.

There may be times you're reading this and think, man, this guy needs to lighten up a bit! To that I say Jordan, keep pushing us. Don't let us get to the end of our lives and wish we would have pursued the dreams that were planted within us from the beginning of our lives.

You know yourself better than anyone else. The problem is, you probably listen to what others say about you more than you listen to yourself. As we age, we let the dreams we are born with die a slow death. We listen to others, we emulate others, and we doubt ourselves. Somehow we have to realize we will only succeed when we become who we were meant to be, not who someone else wishes we would be.

This book will serve as a catalyst for you if you put in the work of doing the things Jordan recommends. He walks you through a variety of tools to help you get to know yourself better and focus on what you have been uniquely gifted to accomplish. I'm guessing most authors wouldn't suggest you set their book aside and go take a test, but Jordan knows this book will not have the impact he intends it to if you don't spend some time outside of the book doing the hard work of self-discovery. If you follow Jordan's advice, you'll be one day closer to achieving the dream that lies inside of you.

Jordan wraps up this book by helping you visualize and assemble your "Life Purpose Puzzle." Just as Bronco helped his friends find and complete their puzzle, Jordan wants to help you identify the pieces of your Life Purpose Puzzle so you can successfully live out your Destiny. I truly believe that this book and the tools that Jordan recommends will help you assemble a life well lived.

Here's to the grand party we will have when we get to the end of our lives and can step back and see the one-of-a-kind masterpieces that our lives of purpose have assembled. Thank you for helping us get to the party, Jordan!

—Kevin Howard, a thankful friend of Jordan's

CONTENTS

INTRODUCTION:
PRIMING THE FIRE OF YOUR CATACLYSM

Get excited. You're now invited to the party. It's time to find your puzzle piece.

Your life purpose puzzle piece (your Destiny) is as unique to you as the way you jump out of bed each morning, the crazy sounds you make when you stretch after sitting for too long, or the way you like your eggs. It's something you have to unlock and find for yourself. No one tool, book, or fancy Ted Talk will show you exactly what you are meant to do with your life. But this is okay.

Catalyzing Your Destiny means YOU get to be in charge. Armed with the right information, you get to decide what your purpose is, and you get to make a plan to complete your goals. You get to take the reins of your life and make incredible progress. You get to become your very own Catalyst and live out your unique Destiny.

Is your fire for Destiny heating up? Good. I knew I could count on you.

This book is not just for the student ready for college, the young couple pondering marriage, wannabe parents, or potential retirees. It's exactly what I wish I knew when I was making the first of these major life decisions, but you don't have to be in any specific stage of your life to reach for your Destiny. It's for anyone who is ready to make a major life change and finally live without regret. It's for you if you want more out of life and are itching to get started with living out your best.

Your Destiny is waiting for you whether you're eighteen with a life plan or sixty-five with no idea what to do next. I've written this book to meet you right where you are. All you need is a desire for change, an appetite to take action on what you learn, and the willingness to learn from (and hopefully avoid) my many mistakes.

This book, if you're ready, will arm you with three powerful life lessons. You'll get to know yourself better than you thought possible. You'll uncover the four points of purpose, and you'll complete your very own life purpose worksheet. You'll learn the bread-and-butter approach to making positive life change and getting things done.

As a younger man, I never pondered life's most important questions. I never gave my Destiny a second thought. Heck, I tripped over my own feet daily, got made fun of for having a hanky in my pocket, and thought that wearing gym shorts with a polo was "no big deal." And this wasn't middle school. This was college. Shake my head... I was the opposite of cool.

I stumbled through life until twenty-five and didn't have a clue what I was doing. I tried my best, and I give my younger self too much of a hard time, but I was naïve and ambivalent towards life's bigger questions. I didn't know the answers because I didn't know what to ask! And therein lies the heart of the struggle.

Have you felt the same at some point in your life? Have you felt the crushing weight of glimpsing a future that appears dark, empty, and devoid of meaning? Maybe that's why you picked up this book?

If so, you've come to the right place. Let's get started shall we?

If I Had Only Known

My college guidance counselor wasn't sure what to do with me when I walked into her office one rainy day in late February 2009, confused, and more than a little worried about my future.

"Jordan, you need to pick a major," She told me.

"I just don't know what I want to do," I replied, eyes darting around the room as if something on the wall might finally give me inspiration. No such luck. All I wanted was to get back to my dorm room. I had a date with Destiny and her name was pepperoni pizza and video games...

"You want to know the truth? Nobody really knows what they want to do," she said. "But you can't stay undeclared. You need to pick a major."

I was a year and a half into a private Christian college with no clue what I was doing with my life. Yes, private college. Expensive, brilliant, high-stakes college. Great for kids with a plan for their future, bad for a guy like me. I had no major, no insights into my personality, no true understanding of who I was and what I was meant to do. Ughh. It's moments like these that make me wish someone had popped in and given me advice, handed me a book, or been firm with me to not just make a decision for the sake of making a decision!

Again, no such luck... More on this story later. You'll find out how indecision and ignorance drove me forward. Things have a way of working out, despite quick decisions and misfires, but we are often our own worst enemy, even though we need to learn to be our own best helper. It's my hope and prayer that this book finds you exactly when you need it most. I want to save you from false starts and the enduring pain of life decisions without insight into your unique makeup. I want to help you turn "If I had only known!" into "This makes sense. I got this. Let's do this."

If you discover your unique life purpose, you won't "work" another day in your life. If you learn how to take targeted positive action, you'll crush every goal you set. When more people embrace their inner power, individuality, and unique skills and strengths, the world will be a better place. This is the mission and purpose of this book: to change the world one person, one purpose, and one action plan at a time. I believe it's possible. By the end of these pages, you will too.

The moment you live your life without regrets is the moment you Catalyze Your Destiny. I want this for you. Bad. Do you want it for you?

In this book I'll share three goals, each of which has a corresponding section with short, punchy, and to-the-point chapters. I've laid out your path before you, given you the resources and directions you need, cut the fluff, and empowered you with sprinklings of inspiration. It's time to dig in:

Goal 1: Discover who you are by building a personal identity blueprint.
Goal 2: Reveal your four points of purpose by using a tool called the Ikigai.
Goal 3: Create a 90-day action plan to make massive progress.

Goal One: Discover Who You Are: Create A Personal Identity Blueprint

The privilege of a lifetime is to become who you truly are. —Carl Jung

In the first part of the book, I'll prime you with self-discovery. It's the first step toward understanding and knowing your purpose. Self-discovery will help you become an expert in you. To begin, ask three questions:

1. What does identity mean to me?
2. Do I know who I really am?
3. What self-discovery gaps am I avoiding or need to overcome?

Identity is a complicated arena, but there's no need to make it more difficult than it is. Our identity rests in understanding ourselves to a higher degree. Identity comprises characteristics, traits, and fluid life decisions. It's those unchangeable parts of you, plus the ebbs and flows of growth and life circumstance.

To sum up, you are who you **were,** who you **are,** and who you **want to be.**

Past. Present. Future. Identity is your past self and your current and future you. The good thing? You will get answers to each introspection point when you do the hard work. Who you were need not define who you want to be. Grow with hard work. Refuse to repeat the same mistakes, be who others say you are, or stuck in your current circumstance.

You also don't share your identity with others. You may share parts of your identity, especially if you cheer for a sports team, love Harry Potter, or compete in the Olympics, but that doesn't mean you share your identity with anyone.

A quick Google search shows several other Jordan Rings alive and well. One Jordan Ring was even on the reality TV show *Love Island* (which I haven't seen). But no one is exactly like you. No one has the same combination of giftings, desires, name, purpose, passions and heart. That Jordan Ring from "Love Island"? If he is a writer, loves golden milk lattes, and can't swim, I'll shave my head and grow a beard. Applaud your incredible uniqueness.

Dr. Seuss beautifully said:

"Today you are You, that is truer than true. There is no one alive who is Youer than You."

The key to Catalyzing your Destiny and discovering purpose is to start with yourself. There is only one you. One unique, powerful, and special you. Isn't it time you got to know yourself a bit better? I've never met you, but I know you are amazing. You're reading this book and trying to grow. You're already ahead of most people. You absolutely have what it takes to make something of your life.

Even though the struggle is real, the world desperately needs to hear from you. It needs to see, hear, smell, touch, and taste your creative works. Live your best life. Bravely step forward and shrug off complacency. Don't fear "imposter syndrome." What you bring to the table is a valuable and indispensable contribution to the world. My skills at Halo 2, tennis drop shots, and how to make the perfect poached egg are an integral part of my identity, even if they seem unimportant.

In section one I want you to not only learn more about yourself, I want you to embrace who you are and fall in love with your uniqueness. In six brief chapters, you'll level up in your understanding of who you are. It will take work, but it's worth it.

We'll unpack six questions for self-awareness:

- Why is knowing myself important?
- Why should I choose growth when comfort is comfortable?
- How do I get to know myself at a deeper level?
- How are we different from others, and why does it matter?
- What if, deep down, I don't believe success is possible for me?
- The fire burning within: how do I maintain momentum?

Goal Two: Reveal Your Purpose with the Four Points of Purpose of the Ikigai

It's not enough to have lived. We should be determined to live for something. —Winston S. Churchill

In section two, we'll use the Japanese word "Ikigai" as a framework for discovering purpose. We'll also call it the four points of purpose, and you'll see these terms used interchangeably. It will help you find what you are an expert at that is unique and specific to you. This intersection, this little golden nugget, is a challenging, but necessary first step to clarifying your unique purpose. If the four points align, the Ikigai emerges and you'll be in the sweet spot.

"Ikigai" is loosely translated "happiness in living." It's a Japanese approach to discovering life purpose. Those who live out their Ikigai are passionate in their daily work, contribute to the greater needs of the world, get paid enough to get by, and develop a skill for their passion.

The following diagram shows the Ikigai:

The Ikigai and the Four Points of Purpose

A Japanese Approach to Discovering Life Purpose

Feeling of uselessness. Work doesn't matter.

What You **Love**

Lacking financial security. Unsustainable contentment.

Happy and Productive

Happy and Influential

What You Are **Good** At

Ikigai!

What the World **Needs**

Financial Security and Productive

Influential and Financial Security

What You Can Get **Paid** For

Comfortable with status quo. Not passionate about work.

Lacking skills. Confusion at progress and narrowing of options.

The diagram might seem overwhelming at first, but don't worry, we'll dive into each point in part two. I'll give you practical ways to gain clarity on each point and find your very own Ikigai. Once you master self-discovery, the next natural step is to tie it all together. The Ikigai is just a tool, but it fits perfectly into the context of Catalyzing Your unique Destiny. You'll learn the answers to the following questions:

- How can the ikigai framework help me discover my purpose?
- How do I find my passion?
- What can I contribute to the world?
- What am I good at?
- What can I get paid to do?
- What am I meant to do?
- Is it possible to live out my ikigai? How five everyday heroes live theirs

Remember, *"The world doesn't need another expert, it needs you."*

In his book, *Man's Search for Meaning*,[1] author, and psychologist Viktor E. Frankl said:

"For the meaning of life differs from man to man, from day to day and from hour to hour. What matters, therefore, is not the meaning of life in general but rather the specific meaning of a person's life at a given moment."

Frankl came to this conclusion after suffering for three years in a concentration camp and seeing countless friends and compatriots led to their deaths. I haven't experienced an iota of what Frankl went through, but I agree we each have an individual purpose to discover.

---

[1] Frankl, Viktor E., et al. Man's Search for Meaning. 1st ed., e-book, Beacon Press, 2006.

No one else has your unique combination of talent, effort, skills, abilities, and life experiences. What YOU can teach someone else is 100% unique to you. You may not be the best at anything right now, but you are you and that's what matters most. There are people out there only you can reach. The way you present information, share ideas, discuss challenges, and give advice differs from others. You don't have to have a doctorate, letters after your name, or have a copy of the town key to be an expert. It's attainable by anyone and everyone. You are an expert in something. Finding out that "something" is the magic of the Ikigai and discovering the intersection of the four points of purpose. It isn't easy, but you know that.

The Ikigai is a framework and a tool, but only you are responsible for Catalyzing Your Destiny. Take ownership of what you know to be right and make it work for you. This is NOT a copout, but a truth we will return to again and again. Stop letting other people influence your path negatively. Take intentional steps toward reaching your Destiny now, not later.

I'll say it again because the point is worth making: Don't sleep on figuring out purpose and potential for your life. Get help, certainly. Call a friend to get feedback. But don't think it will come together or just work out someday. Get up every day and put in the hard work. You've got one shot to get it right, don't squander the time.

Goal Three: Launch Into Action and Ignite Your Soul Fire

> *Tomorrow may be a mystery, but Destiny is not. Destiny is a daily decision. Over time, those daily decisions yield compound interest.* —Mark Batterson, *Win the Day*.[2]

---

[2] Batterson, Mark. Win the Day: 7 Daily Habits to Help You Stress Less & Accomplish More. Multnomah, 2020.

Planning is great. Sections one and two focus on learning and discovery and setting yourself up for success. This is where most books stop. It's also where most people stop reading. Don't make this mistake. Skip to the last section right now if you need to. If you learn nothing else in this book, please remember this takeaway: The impetus of growth and success is taking positive and relentless action towards your goals. Reading is not enough without implementing the knowledge. Self-discovery falls short if you don't use the data to change behaviors. It's great to KNOW your purpose, but it's far better to LIVE it out.

Embrace an action bias to move forward. If you are ready to Catalyze your Destiny, be willing to make sacrifices. You'll learn far more with the risks you take than by the ones you don't. Avoid poor decisions through thoughtful research, prayer, and contemplation, but don't wait until you are 100% sure to move forward. You will never be 100% sure.

The key is moving forward and taking action, even when you aren't sure if it will work out. When you lose momentum, you still gain valuable knowledge and understanding. YOu gain insight into what YOU need to do to move forward with success based on what isn't working. Even if you fall flat on your face, lose your job, or miss the mark on your goals, you'll learn what not to do next time.

Of course, we all want to avoid pain and suffering, and learning from my many failures will help you avoid the same, but don't feel discouraged when things don't work out. I wish things were easier, but they aren't. We have to struggle to reach some goals while other goals just work out. The way forward involves work, perseverance, and a bit of luck.

In the final six action-infused chapters of the book, we'll walk through:

- The unstoppable power of desire
- Getting dangerous with a 90-day plan
- Embracing an action bias
- Two tools to crush your 90-day plan
- Overcoming the whirlwind of life
- Putting the pieces of your life purpose puzzle together

As you devour this book in your favorite blue rocking chair, I have five suggestions to keep in mind and ponder as you read:

1. Embrace the unique contribution you will offer the world.
2. Accept yourself as you are. Get to know your personality, define your purpose, and craft an action plan based on your discoveries.
3. Form a lasting desire to live your purpose with intentionality and intensity.
4. Question question question... You will find a ton of questions in this book. You'll want to skip them (I know how it is, I read personal growth books too), but spending a few moments pondering is important in this book. This book is a treatise on you and thus answering the questions is vital to getting to know yourself better.
5. Shrug off stereotypes from yourself and for others. You are UNIQUE and unlike no other. Be a calm and patient man. Be a woman who's the breadwinner for your family. Be someone who always puts others first. Be dangerously you.

This book's goals are lofty. The aim is high and the journey will be long and arduous. It will take a mighty strong desire, an unrelenting will, and an uncanny ability to see the best in yourself.

Are you up for it?

If you're ready to tap into your Destiny, unlock your purpose, and pave the way to self-discovery, strap in and let's turn up the heat.

Action Step: Commit to doing the exercises in this book by checking the box below. Then grab a pen and get ready to write all over this book. (Kindle readers, don't write on your device, follow the link to the book's resources on the next page.)

❑ *I will Catalyze my Destiny with personal-growth exercises, self-awareness activities, and by creating a 90-day action plan.*

CATALYZING YOUR DESTINY STARTS HERE

As a thank you for picking up this book, I have several bonuses to share with you.

You'll find the bonuses in the companion course which will propel you beyond this book and jumpstart your journey to purpose. It's FREE to sign up for.

In the course you'll find video resources, downloads, links to relevant and updated content, and the following bonuses:

Bonus #1: A personal identity blueprint to maximize self-discovery.

Bonus #2: An Ikigai diagram and journal pages to unlock purpose.

Bonus #3: A blank 90-day action-plan template to pursue your Destiny.

To receive your bonuses, sign up for the FREE course by visiting:

https://www.jmring.com/cyd-book/

Immediately after signing up, you'll be emailed direct access to the course.

Enjoy!

PS: Kindle readers, this is where you'll get access to accompanying PDFs and other documents.

PPS: Print book readers, you'll also find the worksheets in the back of this book!

PART ONE:

DISCOVER WHO YOU ARE:
CREATE A PERSONAL IDENTITY BLUEPRINT

CHAPTER ONE: KNOW THYSELF AND THRIVE

Aristotle once said:

"Knowing yourself is the beginning of all wisdom."

Wisdom is born out of understanding. It starts with knowing yourself first. Your impact on the world around you will be limited if you don't first get to know the one person you are most suited to get to know: You!

Do you know who you are? I mean, do you *really* know who you are? Most of us think we know, but don't actually have a clue. This includes me at various times in my life...

"I'll choose... Criminal justice! Sounds good, right? Can I go now? I'm late for my ultimate frisbee game."

I wish I picked my college major out of a hat. It might have turned out better. Two of my good friends, Tim and Mike, had already chosen criminal justice as their college major. They both wanted to be police officers. This was never my intention. I wanted to... What? I had no idea... So I picked it too. It made sense for them, so why wouldn't it work for me?

My guidance counselor, bless her, was as relieved as I was. She was now free from trying to help this confused college sophomore figure out what to do next. I don't blame her. I was clueless with a stubborn confidence. Not a great combination.

I went back to my dorm, fired up the Xbox, grabbed some Mountain Dew, and settled in for the easy path, never stopping to second guess my decision but plowing forth toward the goal. This relentless spirit is one of my favorite things about myself but, mixed with immaturity and decisions lacking the right clarity, it came with a high cost.

It's not without a touch of sadness and regret that I look back at these lost years. Yes, I made some amazing friends, met my wife, and upped my Halo skill level, but I could have been so much more. I could have taken advantage of an excellent study-abroad program, invested in community-building projects, or taken challenging courses. Instead, I wasted time, skipped far too many classes, and was ultimately less than what I could have been.

I share this story to illustrate three key points:

1. Picking a direction is good, but without understanding the deeper *why* we might get lost along the way.
2. Sometimes the euphoria of choosing a path clouds our judgement on the rightness of the decision.
3. If we don't stop to analyze our current path, we might drift from our purpose.

I was just a kid in college, so I know I shouldn't be too hard on myself, but I can't help but wish I had known myself better. It would have caused me to question how any job in the criminal justice and sociology field would work for me. Did I really want to be a cop, a therapist, a judge or a chief? No. I never did.

I value the determination I displayed in my youth. It's almost always better to decide quickly and get to work vs. floundering and second guessing. But I was basing the efficacy of my decision on very little information, and once made, I didn't count the continuing cost, nor did I think to pivot.

I should have asked myself better questions like: How would earning a degree in criminal justice move me forward on the right path? What exercises could have helped me to see my own flaws in reasoning? Instead of asking myself, *"What do I want to do with my life?"* A much better question would have been, *"Who am I?"*

Starting with *"Who am I"* is infinitely better. Yes, we can be just about anything we want, but we weren't created with the ability to do anything and everything. Contrary to popular opinion, you shouldn't be whatever you want to be. Certainly, you *can* be and do whatever you want, but if your choice doesn't fit your unique makeup, you won't be able to maximize your potential and your life's adventure will have far too many rides on the struggle bus. I should do only what I am meant to do. There is a unique purpose only I can fulfill. The same goes for you.

To figure out the meaning of life, start with determining who you are. Start with your unique giftings, abilities, strengths, talents, personality, etc. There is no one-size-fits-all option for these personality markers. No one can tell you exactly who you are, but it's there for *you* to uncover. The good news is this section of the book will guide you on this path towards uncovering personal identity.

We have to determine our life path, make hard decisions, and ultimately find meaning within the grander scheme. Collective purposes such as ending slavery worldwide, reducing human trafficking, or granting free access to healthcare to all 7+ billion of us are incredible, but when you break these goals down, you'll find separate duties, responsibilities, and gaps needing the best person available. To be the best person for the job, know thyself. Know why you are the way you are before making major life decisions. Don't be like me...

Besides having almost no idea what I wanted to do in college, I didn't know myself very well. I wasn't even self-aware enough to recognize the negative impact a diet full of pizza, Mountain Dew, and late-night cereal was having on my body. The slow onslaught of poor decisions is tough to avoid, because you don't see it until it's too late. It's hard to sum up my college self in a few sentences, but here goes:

Jordan was a nice guy who was always ready to listen and understand. He was self-assured, but lacking confidence beneath the surface. He didn't believe he could do anything he wanted. Unbeknownst to him, he was resigned to living a life others expected of him. He was a good friend, but his lack of self-awareness and focus cost him dearly in terms of productivity and success.

Now, if someone had told me this, I would have lost it. I appeared confident, but deep down, I was lost and confused. I wasn't fully cognizant of my identity, had little understanding of my skills, and wasn't doing anything to develop my personality. I'm going to give college Jordan a break here so he can wipe his tears, and jump ahead a few years to point to the power of self-knowledge.

Fast forward to when I turned twenty-five. I was feeling okay with my life, but it was the type of "okay" that's not really okay. Can you relate? I was pondering my life and meaning. Feelings of inadequacy, uselessness, and exposed apathy were bubbling to the surface. Then I attended the Global Leadership Summit through my work, and everything changed for the better. This experience ignited the fire of personal growth in my heart and soul.

I dove into reading and two specific books propelled me forward: *In a Pit with a Lion on a Snowy Day* by Mark Batterson, and *Crush It* by

Gary Vaynerchuk altered my life's direction. A book by a lesser-known pastor, and a book by a leading social media business expert combined to launch my rocket on its journey, and I've never looked back. The books hit me with a double portion of self-awareness and the excitement of future possibilities. It was like a switch suddenly turned on in my brain. I was, for lack of a better word, enlightened. I've been running a race ever since by doing my best to improve myself, create content that helps others, and live without regrets. I Catalyzed my Destiny, and I didn't even know it.

Looking at the amount of growth I've achieved since college is exciting. I'm nowhere near perfect, but I like my current self a heck of a lot better than college Jordan. And I think I'm going to like future Jordan even better too. The key to this growth? Self-awareness, clarity, hustle, and relentless effort. You'll learn strategies for each in this book.

If college Jordan read this book and it pushed him toward the messy, brutal, and painfully eye-opening process of self-discovery, he might have tossed it in the garbage. If I were standing there, I would have asked him two questions that I'll ask you as well:

1. *"Do you want a simple life or a purpose-filled life?"*
2. *"Do you want to play it safe or live dangerously?"*

There is no middle ground on the journey of life. There is no neutral ground; you're either falling back or moving forward. If you take the painful route of self-discovery and do the exercises within this book, it will hurt. If you are a sensitive type like me, you might even cry. But that's okay. As we'll learn, pain is part and parcel to self-discovery and personal growth.

Be the phoenix rising from the ashes of your past self. Thrust off your false self and get REAL with who you are.

According to Dale Carnegie we spend 95% of our time thinking about ourselves. We might as well use this valuable time to think more deeply about who we really are and who we desire to become.

But what areas of self-discovery and reflection are important? It turns out, several. We'll spend a few brief paragraphs on each area below. As you read, think about how you do in each of the self-discovery realms. Do you know where you stand? Do you measure up to the person you want to be? Could you be better than you are now?

The following gut checks will lay the foundation of your journey to Destiny. Determine your baseline and then climb.

Areas for Self-Discovery and Reflection

Spiritual Discovery

It's incumbent upon us all to at least know how we feel about spirituality. Spirituality matters more than we might realize. Even if you shun spiritual belief and prefer a more grounded approach to life, you'll run into others with strong spiritual beliefs. You should understand what you believe and how important it is for interpersonal interactions. The only wrong path is not picking one at all.

Conducting a spiritual gut check can be painful, but it's needed. Are you right with your maker? Have you spent time in meditation and/or prayer? What is your spiritual creed and are you following it? You can choose not to believe in a higher power, but do you have a potent reason not to?

Spiritual discovery is first because it forms the bottom of the pyramid for everything you do next. We won't dive into it too much in this book because it's not an easy topic, nor am I an expert, but knowing your spiritual beliefs (or lack thereof) is vital for determining your purpose and living your best life.

Christianity informs and directs my purpose. Maybe an intense love of animals informs yours. I'm also a huge proponent of putting people first and showing love. You won't find me judging your lifestyle or choices. My biggest fear is that a reader, a friend, or a new acquaintance would see me as someone who thinks too highly of himself. Knowing this fear helps me to remember not to take myself seriously and to make fun of myself when appropriate. The only thing I'm truly confident about is that if I make my mom's famous homemade bread, you'll love it.

My love for people fuels my purpose of helping individuals find their unique contribution. A book on purpose would be incomplete without this important note: Your purpose is incomplete if not based on something bigger than yourself. Know where you stand spiritually and infuse it with your greater life purpose.

Health and Wellness Check

Did you know you can push yourself far beyond what you think you're capable of? The human body is capable of impressive feats. Just ask anyone who's climbed Mt. Everest, stepped out onto the surface of the moon, or eaten an entire sleeve of Oreos in one sitting. You can rise above whatever limits you've imposed on yourself, and that includes your physical well-being.

The first place to start is analyzing your tendency to veg out in front of a screen. As a nation and as a society, we spend far too much time in front of the TV and other screens. In fact, serious cognitive decline[3] occurs when watching TV beyond 3.5 hours a day. It kills me to say it as a huge Dwight Schrute fan, but binge watching *The Office* is not a healthy practice.

During the COVID-19 pandemic, my wife and I had more meals together than ever before. We watched our fair share of television in the early stages, but eventually regularly ate meals together with no electronics. Turns out talking to my best friend is a lot of fun, and I'm glad we transitioned.

Health and wellness is something we can't afford to ignore. Our health rises and falls on the backs of our decisions. Do I eat out or cook a healthy meal? Should I go for a walk or take a nap? Do I really need to eat fruits and veggies!? Our health and wellness directly affect our energy levels, and how much we have to give. You might be a banana and a glass of water away from realizing your potential for the day. It's incredibly simple but ridiculously powerful.

I ask myself three questions when I am feeling down or anxious:

1. Did I pray about this?
2. Did I drink a full glass of water recently?
3. Did the last meal I ate include a superfood?

Self-discovery in the health and wellness realm means analyzing your tendencies and patterns to learn where you fail. It's about learning where you are today and making a plan for a healthier future by making small positive decisions.

---

[3] Fancourt, Daisy, and Andrew Steptoe. "Television Viewing and Cognitive Decline in Older Age: Findings from the English Longitudinal Study of Ageing." Scientific Reports, 28 Feb. 2019, www.nature.com/articles/s41598-019-39354-4.

Relational: Who's Mad at You Today?

At any given time of day, there's always someone who's waiting on me for a response. Lest you think I'm a busy or popular person (I'm neither), it's no one's fault but mine. I get overwhelmed by continuing a conversation. I often leave people hanging because my energy's worn out. Some people really don't like this.

As an INFJ on the Myers-Briggs (more on this in chapter three) I struggle with feeling like I let people down. Members of the INFJ group struggle (to varying degrees) with keeping up with people and responding to messages. We can't be everything to everybody, but often we feel like we should be. Thus, limiting our relational growth to a select few is a good strategy.

You cannot judge your success or failure as a person on global metrics. Instead, judge yourself based on what you know to be true of you. You know yourself better than most; what's a character flaw you need to be more aware of or embrace?

I'm not someone who can maintain a high level of relational stability with too many people. I'm apt to keep a few friends and colleagues and hold them close. For me, if those close relationships have issues, I know I need to dive in and get to work. If several people who aren't in my close circle are waiting on me for a response, well sucks to be you. Just kidding (sort of), but I can't hold myself to an unreasonable standard. I've learned to pick my battles. It's not about creating excuses; it's about knowing yourself to a higher degree, getting better, but also cutting yourself slack when you need it.

Education: What Do You Know?

Charlie "Tremendous" Jones says:

"You will be the same person in five years as you are today except for the people you meet and the books you read."

Focusing on people is important, but so too is what you take in for knowledge. What books do you want to have read in five years? The best-kept secret to staying educated and at the top of your game is that you don't know what you don't know. Reading books all the way through (no summary cheating!) sheds light on subjects you didn't even know you needed to care about. As you read this book you'll pick up one or two things you didn't previously know, and learn a few new life tidbits. Every book has at least one or two golden nuggets waiting for you to uncover.

I have a huge list of must-read books you'll find in the resources section of the companion course. Read the following books first if you haven't already:

- *How to Win Friends and Influence People* by Dale Carnegie
- *Think and Grow Rich* by Napoleon Hill
- *The Art of Non-Conformity* by Chris Guillebeau
- *Man's Search for Meaning* by Viktor E. Frankl
- *Love Does* by Bob Goff
- *Factfulness* by Hans Rosling

Reading isn't the only path to knowledge, but it's the most effective. Online courses, YouTube, traditional education, coaching, mentoring, etc., are great ways to learn too, but nothing beats a well-researched and impactful book for deep learning. And that's this author's completely unbiased opinion.

Future Goals: What Do I Want to Do?

We'll discuss this realm later on with the refreshing life goals exercise, but what you want to do with your life is an important part of who you are. Yesterday doesn't exist anymore. There's only this moment right now and your plans for the future. Who do you want to be tomorrow, in a week, five years from now?

Don't worry. You don't need to have an answer ready to go. Merely pondering and then making plans with your ponderance is the key.

The French writer Antoine de Saint-Exupéry said:

"A goal without a plan is just a wish."

Indeed!

There is little of more importance than self-discovery. It leads you to greater understanding in spiritual matters and renewed health and wellness aims, guides you toward truth in how you interact with others, shows you what you still need to learn and where you need to grow, and leads you on a wild ride of purposeful fulfillment in life by defining your personal identity and setting powerful goals.

Why would you choose to be anything else when you can choose to be you?

Action Step: Of the above personal growth areas, which ones do you need to work on? Which ones are going great and you want to maintain? Sum up your current situation in a few sentences.

_____

_____

_____

30

CHAPTER TWO: CHOOSING PAIN

I chose pain over comfort on the following three life occasions, and each time it served me well.

In 2015, my wife and I moved from Pennsylvania to North Carolina. A new state, new job, new people, new life. Nothing could have prepared us for the change. But we welcomed it, looked forward to it, accepted and embraced it. We started our new life working at three different retirement communities over the course of two years.

In 2019, we dipped our toes into the digital nomad lifestyle and spent two months in Thailand. The smells assaulted us, the sights astounded, and the food, although delicious, was foreign. It was challenging, exciting, and worth every second. It whetted an appetite and ignited a craving for seeing the world and experiencing things we never imagined. It became the Catalyst for our desire to become full-time digital nomads.

At the end of 2019, we moved from home to nowhere. 2020 was our year. The dream was to see a different country every month or two. We gave away our furniture, sold all of our belongings, and packed two backpacks to see the world. Covid-19 hit and changed everything. Lisbon, Portugal went from our first stop to second home. We adapted and thrived.

Looking back, there isn't a single thing I'd change about the decisions I've made in the last six years. I've been living forward, and

I can honestly say it's been worth every second. It hasn't worked out exactly as I planned, nor has it been easy, but such is life, and such is the vastness of possibility when choosing the foreign and the uncomfortable. It might suck, but you grow through it.

It was worth the roof rat parade and food poisoning in Thailand. It was worth months of lockdown in Lisbon. It was worth the tears, time, and turbulence during our days as assistant community managers in North Carolina. The pain, the struggles, and the harrowing moments were all worth it because they helped form the person I am today. I'm still growing, but these adventures were worth the cost of blood, sweat, and tears for the opportunity to experience life to the fullest.

I love Netflix weekends as much as the average millennial, but growth doesn't come through sameness and comfort. Growth occurs when you get outside the door and get walking. We build memories when we seek change and adventure. We fully live only when we choose pain over comfort. Choose to live outside of your comfort zone and thrive.

This chapter will teach you how to choose pain over ease and comfort. It's not an easy read, but it's an important truth. It's a necessary step before we dive into tools to get to know ourselves. Sameness and comfort kill. Adventure and pain grow. "No pain, no gain" might be a cliche, but it's a mantra we should embrace daily.

I don't need to convince you of the importance of change and growth. You know this. It's why you picked up a book called *Catalyze Your Destiny*. We all know this intrinsically, but it's been squeezed out of us by modern success metrics and a busy lifestyle. It's the goal of this book to get you to choose what's hard over what's easy. Success comes when you do the thing no one else is doing. If it were easy, everyone would do it. Choose the path that's rocky and uphill.

If you have a high-paying job, a big house, and a happy family, you've achieved the American dream. But the American dream doesn't lead to happiness. It can be part of the journey, but the lie is that it's the last rung on the ladder. These metrics don't lead to lasting happiness. At the time of this writing, Americans are the unhappiest they've been in nearly 50 years.[4] Only by understanding unique identity and purpose can we be truly happy.

Are you happy? Never mind what the studies say, how are *you* doing? Most of us are chasing happiness in all the wrong ways because of false assumptions, comfort, security, peace, and ease. These are basic needs we strive to meet but are not the right end goals. We treat peace and security as the end of all goals. We think they will lead us to happiness. But they don't. Comfort, security, and wealth won't lead us where we actually want to go.

The fundamental problem is that human beings are insatiable. We always want more of what is just beyond our reach. But this is extremely dangerous. If we chase the wrong things, no matter how grand they seem, we will only find disappointment when we reach them. More often than not, what we think we want isn't what we actually need. I learned this the hard way.

What I Thought I Wanted

Beach. Flexibility. Private hotels. Friends. Peace. Love. Simple work. No pain. No demands. No problems. Complete and utter freedom.

Freedom, to a digital nomad and entrepreneur, is everything. We want the ultimate say in our schedules and 100% control of our time.

---

[4] Associated Press. "Americans Are the Unhappiest They've Been in 50 Years, Poll Finds." NBC News, 16 June 2020, www.nbcnews.com/politics/politics-news/americans-are-unhappiest-they-ve-been-50-years-poll-finds-n1231153.

We desire control above all else. We want ultimate freedom without the problem of commitment. But freedom doesn't lead to happiness. We can't be free in every way. We will always be slaves to time, our bodies, and Mother Nature, and nothing could have shed light on the fallacy of nomadic freedom like COVID-19. All at once, the desire for freedom came crashing down with the threat of a worldwide pandemic.

Without the allure of constant travel, I had to face my Destiny. I had to have some tough conversations with myself about what I was doing and why. It led me down the path of writing this book and realigning my life goals. It was a painful process of self-discovery that was full of false starts and failures, but it was essential for my growth journey. Failure is how I've learned to learn.

What I thought I wanted was ultimate freedom. What I really wanted was to fill most of my time with purpose and giving back. With the rising of the morning sun comes the chance to win the day. You don't need to have it all figured out, just be better than you were yesterday.

The recent COVID-19 pandemic brought to life the question of what we truly want out of life. No one could escape the challenges it brought. It left no one unscathed. The world changed overnight. Life is amazing, but it's also ridiculously fragile.

My parents and younger brother live in Maine, where the power goes out frequently because of inclement weather. What do we do with ourselves when the power goes out? It's challenging for some and maddening for others. So, what do you really want out of life? What truly matters?

Your purpose and what you want will be unique to you. Your life direction is your choice. How to pursue your journey is up to you.

But I implore you to choose the pain of self-reflection and growth. If not, pain will choose you. There's no escaping death. No way out of our final journey. In the immortal words of Tony Stark, *"Part of the journey is the end."*

Choose the pain of doing the hard work. Choose the pain of turning your phone off for a weekend. Choose the pain of quitting your job to pursue your passion and purpose. Choose the pain of analyzing what you really want out of life and reaching for it. Choose the pain of ignoring your own needs for a day to give back instead.

Life isn't easy. You can make it easier, but only for a time. Every second you spend searching for comfort, looking for methods to ease pain, or conforming to how the world says you should live, is time wasted. Pain will find you anyway, embrace the suck instead.

There will be several transitional points in your life. Will you choose what's easy or what's hard? Will you choose the pain of writing your novel or the comfort of watching TV? Will you choose to read the rest of this book or eat the last piece of cake in your fridge? Will you help your neighbor move, call your grandma, or make a meal for a hurting friend? Or will your life look like what happens when you leave the metal spoon in your coffee when you heat it in the microwave? Oops.

Choosing what's easy over what's right is a sign of immaturity. I still do it way too often. The cake never makes it to my fridge. I eat it all instead. Every bite. But imagine how it'll feel when I return from a six-hour flight and find there's no cake... When I choose the rocky path over the paved one, I grow along the way. Every time I choose to save the cake for tomorrow, I experience a not insignificant victory in delayed gratification and willpower.

If we hadn't moved away from friends and family to a painful job, we wouldn't have broken out of our shells. If we hadn't braved the otherworldliness of Thailand, we wouldn't have caught the travel bug. If we hadn't embraced the unknown, a wild zest for life and adventure wouldn't have filled our souls.

Nothing good comes from turning down the more challenging course of action. My favorite stories are of friends who quit their jobs to seek more, not because quitting is the goal, but because so much good will come from embracing a new challenge. I'm not worried that it will be hard for them. I KNOW it will be a challenging, painful, and crazy ride. Despite difficulties and challenges, growth trumps comfort and sameness. Choosing pain always leads to growth. Growth is an invaluable resource you never lose. I want this for you. It always stays with you and is worth more than gold or convenience.

Analyzing Roots: The 5 Whys

As you *"seek to know thyself,"* and come across potentially painful life crossroads where you need to make important decisions, ask *5 whys* for the problem you face. Picture explaining your problem to a toddler who will invariably ask "but why?" to each of your standard responses. Don't respond with "because I said so." Instead, dig in and answer honestly. We should continually ask ourselves these questions for any problem we face. We should always grow and pivot as needed. What do you really want? What's holding you back? What's stopping you from living out your potential?

Sakichi Toyoda, the Japanese industrialist, inventor, and founder of Toyota Industries, developed the 5 Whys technique in the 1930s.[5]

---

[5] "5 Whys: Getting to the Root of a Problem Quickly." Mind Tools, 2020, www.mindtools.com/pages/article/newTMC_5W.htm.

It's a valuable tool to help you dive into your personal why. It takes a little work, but asking why five times solves the problem of knowing when to choose the pain. If the end "why" is to help you grow as a person, it will almost always be worth it to say yes and go for it. If the "why" doesn't relate to your mission or purpose, reconsider the priority of solving the problem in question.

When you answer why at each level, dig deeper. This is a great way to solve problems because it helps you see where things go wrong. It's also a way to mull over life's biggest questions by exposing the root issues. Asking why tears away layers until there is nothing left to hide behind. No excuses remain to impede you from facing your Destiny and choosing the more painful but beneficial path.

This process is childlike but helpful. Little Billy is looking at you with wide eyes and a Cheshire cat grin asking, "but why!?" repeatedly. Remember, you can't say, "Just because I said so," after the second why. Answer and answer honestly.

Here's an example of a problem drilled with why's:

Problem: Janet Dawson hates her job.

"Why?"

Because Janet is unfulfilled, unmotivated, and bored.

"Why?"

Because Janet isn't in the right fit and doesn't know what she wants to do.

"Why?"

Because Janet hasn't spent the time to figure out her Destiny and life goals.

"Why?"

Because Janet is busy and hasn't prioritized her life by asking the big life questions.

"Why?"

Because Janet hasn't Catalyzed her Destiny.

Potential solutions for Janet:

- Read this book (and others!) all the way to the end.
- Talk to a close friend about steps she could take.
- Consider what she really wants from a career and choose one that reflects this.
- Make a new life plan and work on it day by day.
- Find new motivation to work at her current job and turn it into something she loves.

Diving deep and continually asking why will force your genuine desires to the surface. This is the only way you can know why you take certain actions. It's the only way you can Catalyze Your Destiny. Ask why, expose your roots, and rebuild. This childlike lens will show you a mirror into your future. You won't be able to hide behind excuses anymore. Beware. Solutions take time; nothing happens overnight. In his book *Start with Why*[6] Simon Sinek shares more on the importance of knowing your why:

People don't buy what you do; they buy why you do it. And what you do simply proves what you believe.

This applies as aptly for the common person as it does for the

---

[6] Sinek, Simon. Start with Why: How Great Leaders Inspire Everyone to Take Action. Illustrated, e-book, Portfolio, 2011.

business professional. Knowing why you do what you do is infinitely more important than knowing the what. We can spend all of our time ferreting around worrying about the what and the how, but wrestling with our why is much more effective.

Here's another big-picture example:

Problem: I'm not happy.

"Why?"

"Because I have no friends, no hobbies, and no money."

"Why?"

"Well, I'm not really a good friend myself, I don't like to do things, and I haven't found a job I'm good at."

"Why?"

"I guess I never learned how to be a good friend, I'm afraid to try new things, and I'm not a hard worker."

"Why?"

"Because I'm lazy and don't take the time to improve."

"Why?"

"Because I don't believe in myself…"

Potential solutions:

- Put yourself outside your comfort zone more often.
- Make a list of ways you can give back and/or repair old friendships.
- Build your self-esteem by reading life-changing books.

- Make a list of jobs you'd enjoy and research the steps to landing one.
- Start a side hustle and support yourself using your passions.
- Practice simple happiness exercises, such as smiling or basking in the warmth of the sun.

This example is one of many possibilities in how this exercise could play out, but the important part is to shed light on areas of specific improvement. It's much easier to solve the problem of being a better friend than solving the nebulous problem of general unhappiness.

I encourage you to try it by analyzing one of your most annoying recurring problems or goals. And brace yourself: We'll continue to practice these sorts of deep dives throughout the book. Even if you feel great and are doing well, you might benefit from this process. Eat some humble pie and try it out.

The process is painful and never easy, but choosing pain is one key to Catalyzing Your Destiny. Are you ready to take the next steps and unleash chaos against the old you? Good. I thought you'd be up for it.

Action step: Apply the "why?" question five times to your current roadblock. Come on, you knew this was coming. Dig deep until you get to the root issue. Don't stop until you come up with a list of solutions. Take action in real life even though it's painful.

Problem or Tricky Goal

_____

_____

_____

Why?

_____

Why?

_____

Why?

_____

Why?

_____

Why?

_____

Possible Solutions:

_____

_____

_____

CHAPTER THREE: 10 TOOLS FOR SELF-DISCOVERY

A lemon seed, planted in the ground, will only ever become a lemon tree. It might want to be a lime, but no matter how angry it gets, it won't be able to turn green. A lemon seed has it easy. It doesn't have to think about what it is and what it wants to become, it just is. You are infinitely more complex than a lemon seed, but trying to be something you're not is not only dangerous for you, it will prevent the fruit of your maximum potential from changing the world.

In a world filled with over seven billion people, personality is a superpower. Each person is unique and important, yet as a group we follow collective traits. Some people are naturally quiet, while others are boisterous. Some are always lost in thought, while others stop to smell every flower. Some easily make decisions, while others agonize over every possibility.

The right path to personal identity is holistic, individualistic, and personal. No one test, experiment, or activity is enough. You are the sum of many parts. The risk of taking the tests I'll share below is getting locked into a label. But you are NOT the test; the test gives you language to understand yourself and others. This is critical to unlocking and understanding identity. It's up to you to rise above the comfort of belonging to the painful process of acceptance of who you are.

You are NOT the test. You are the sum of the whole, uniquely created for a specific purpose and with a personal identity. Let's find out what that is, together. In this chapter, ten tools and exercises form the backbone of self-discovery. You'll find these experiments more than satisfactory to get started on the road to understanding more about yourself.

The following exercises made an enormous difference in my personal growth. The insights helped me greatly in understanding myself and others. These ten tools may or may not work for you, but at the very least, you'll know who you aren't. At their absolute failure point, you'll at least get to think about who you are. This is the often-misunderstood part of self-discovery that's actually a golden nugget: A test can give you "wrong" answers, and you might still learn something new.

Before we go any further, let's talk about the elephant in the room. There are very smart people (read: smarter than me) who think personality tests are a dime a dozen and worthless. One such expert, Benjamin Hardy, Ph.D., doesn't believe in the power of personality tests like the MBTI or Enneagram. He says in his book *Personality Isn't Permanent*:[7]

"Type-based personality tests like Myers-Briggs, DISC, and Enneagram are junk science. There is no such thing as a personality "type." That's a gross oversimplification and stereotype that leads to mindlessness, both about yourself and other people."

Talk about throwing out the wine with the cork!

Despite the above, I rather enjoyed Hardy's book. He makes excellent points of not labeling people, being careful about limiting ourselves, and focusing more on who we want to be rather than who we were. But, in throwing out so-called "junk science," Dr. Hardy

---

[7] Hardy, Benjamin. Personality Isn't Permanent: Break Free from Self-Limiting Beliefs and Rewrite Your Story. e-book, Portfolio, 2020.

has missed the tremendous opportunity these tools provide: self-discovery through a common lens. By looking at commonalities, discovering patterns, and assembling the puzzle pieces into their complete whole, we'll gain a deeper understanding of people and the world. Many still use these tools today to gain insight into personal understanding, and it's why I give them my personal seal of approval for getting started.

There are literally thousands of tools out there, but I've chosen these ten to get you started on the road to self-discovery. These tools will give you insights into your strengths, expose your weaknesses, and will put you on the path to discovering what the heck you are doing here on this Earth.

Even if you're the most self-aware person out there, swallow a hearty piece of humble pie and do the work. I find something new about myself every time I complete a new test. I don't always like what I find, but the pain is worth learning more about myself. Choose the painful road of self-discovery and bravely question who you are.

This chapter is action-oriented. As you read, pause and do the exercises, or make a mental note of the tools you would like to come back to at a later date. Nothing you read will be as powerful as insights gained from personal reflection, constructive feedback, and individual coaching. I'm giving you the tools; use them as you see fit.

This section is most powerful if you write your answers as you go. Remember, you can follow the link below to sign up for your free personal identity blueprint (or see the back of this book), and get access to further resources, test links, and resource recommendations for all ten tools below (plus even more tools for the ultra curious).

https://www.jmring.com/cyd-book/

Self-Discovery Tools

Henry Ford shares:

"Thinking is the hardest work there is, which is probably the reason so few engage in it."

Don't just read this chapter and move on. Think, consider, and take action. I won't beat you over the head with the action hammer (but don't tempt me!), but writing your answers is a bold action step that 93% of other readers won't take. Set yourself apart by doing the hard work.

Remain open to the process and your business will boom, your relationships will strengthen, and your personal growth will explode upward. It takes doing the challenging and rigorous work of introspection. Channel a keen and careful Sherlock Holmes eye for detail and mix it with a dash of Elon Musk's futuristic zest for the possible.

1) Ask Five Friends One Question

The first self-discovery tool is an icebreaker, but it's also the most valuable. Reach out to five of your closest friends and say something like:

"This is random, but a book I'm reading prompted me to pose this question to a close friend: What do you see as my personal strengths? What is a trait or characteristic unique to me? All feedback is welcome. Thank you! I appreciate your time."

I used this exact message when reaching out to a close friend, and it spawned a great conversation. He not only sent me encouraging and positive feedback, I did the same for him. Jot down what people say back to you and ponder the implications.

You want to know the sad truth? We rarely get to tell people how we really feel. How regrettable is that? Open up the doors of opportunity by using this step to talk to people at a deeper level. The good that can come out of these conversations is astounding, and it will set you on the right path.

Asking for feedback is tough, but this exercise works. Try it and see what conversations you can strike up. Consider what you can give back and don't be afraid to lift others up too. The power of this exercise is that it's wrapped in positivity. You're not asking for constructive criticism or negative feedback, you're asking for confirmation of your most likeable traits.

2) Take the MBTI Personality Test

It's beauty that captures your attention; personality that captures your heart. –Oscar Wilde.

Personality tests give you previously unknown or misunderstood insights about yourself and others. They are valuable for better understanding who you are to your core. You can change and grow, but there are certain characteristics you needn't be afraid to accept and embrace. The Myers-Briggs Type Indicator (MBTI) personality test is one of the best tools for explaining how people are different. It's helped millions of people to better understand their parents, spouses, family, coworkers, friends, and themselves.

What you can learn from the test is profound. What you are looking for is knowledge, and the words to express this information in understandable and relatable ways.

Some people avoid these types of tests like the plague because of the fear of being labeled. As mentioned previously, Benjamin Hardy thinks it's "junk science." But its utility lies in what you do considering the information and the results. I won't dive too deep into the history of this specific test, other than to say it gets its roots from the psychologist Carl Jung. The mother-and-daughter team of Katharine Cook Briggs and Isabel Briggs Myers took hold of Jung's theories and created the MBTI.

There are sixteen personality types, made up of four different letter pairs. We are mixes of these, and it's rare to be a pure type (meaning I'm an INFJ most days but dip into the traits of other types sometimes).

We won't cover each of the 16 types, but here are the four dichotomies in brief:

Introvert (I) vs. Extravert (E) —Where you get your energy

- Introverts get energy from being alone and do best by internally processing before interacting.
- Extraverts get energy from other people out in the world.

Pro tip: Extraverts, ask an introverted friend to coffee (they want you to ask!). Introverts, say yes to the invitation.

Intuitive (N) vs. Sensing (S) —How we process information

- Intuition is pondering life, thinking deeply, and living in the future.
- Sensing is observing and living in the now. Facts-based.

Pro tip: Intuitives, stop putting the weight of the world on your shoulders. Sensors, consider the future of humanity and what you are most looking forward to.

Thinking (T) vs. Feeling (F) —How we make decisions

- Thinkers use logic and analytics first.
- Feelers use what they feel, and how others feel, to make decisions.
- Both types use a mix of logic and feelings, but the degree of use varies.

Pro tip: Feelers, don't be afraid to make decisions because it "feels right." Thinkers, exercise your logic and move forward with confidence.

Perceiving (P) vs. Judging (J) —Our approach to work, planning, and daily operations

- Perceivers love possibilities, are great at improvising, and prefer to keep their options open. They show up to the party whenever.
- Judgers are schedulers, highly organized, and prefer structure and planning. Judgers show up exactly on time to any party.

Pro tip: Perceivers, say yes right now and move forward on your next decision point. Judgers, stop and wait a full day before saying yes to the next invite, event, or work project.

For more information and to take the MBTI test for free online, go here to access the companion course for this book: https://www.jmring.com/cyd-book/

3) CliftonStrengths

Knowing my strengths taught me the value of doubling down on what I'm good at and getting help with my weaknesses. It's also helped me become a better author and content marketer. Gallup CliftonStrengths provides insights on how I can infuse my writing with what I'm good at, and it has since become one of my favorite communication superpowers to have in my back pocket.

I realize I can't reach everybody, nor should I try. I infuse my writing style with feeling and vulnerability, which some won't like. This is okay. Instead of overwhelming with data, I'll write to encourage and uplift. Instead of long discussions on the power of habits for small gains, I'll dive deeper into purpose. Instead of influencing decisions, I'll share my story and invite you to come along for the ride. I don't write to everybody. I write to the type of person best suited to be impacted by my words and style. Hopefully that's you.

CliftonStrengths is a test you can take online, which primarily shows you what you are good at. It doesn't focus on your negative areas and weaknesses. Instead, it provides a framework of 34 signature themes (also called strengths) and ranks you by the themes in which you show the most promise. The test is not free, but it's a very impactful tool to determine what you are best suited for.

Your signature themes can fall into four major domains: **Executing, Influencing, Relationship Building, and Strategic Thinking**. Here is a summary of the four domains:

- Executing: People who rank high in executing themes get things done efficiently and effectively.
- Influencing: People with high influencing themes are great at winning others over and sharing and spreading ideas.
- Relationship Building: High Relationship Building themes exist in those who emphasize people and nurturing relationships.

- Strategic Thinking: People who are strong in Strategic Thinking always have a plan and thrive on creating the best outcomes.

View your top five strengths as the things you can't *not* do. Your top five strengths are what you do naturally, and when you do them, you light up. Your strengths should match what you already know about yourself, but will also provide insights into the activities you need to keep doing.

You'll find knowing your strengths useful for getting to know yourself better. The insights it provides are sometimes surprising, yet disturbingly accurate. When you take the test, invest in the resources Gallup provides to further your strength development.

Here are my top five strengths:

1. Futuristic
2. Empathy
3. Connectedness
4. Relator
5. Strategic

Living life by following your strengths not only informs your Destiny, it makes your day-to-day life more enjoyable and impactful. Futuristic matches my high intuition from the MBTI (the N in the INFJ). I'm constantly processing life in the abstract big picture. When I'm firing on all cylinders it means I'm dreaming big and making big life goals. When I'm not exercising my number one strength I'm too focused on present realities, and anxiety and depression gain a stronger foothold on my life.

Combining my top five strengths shows that my futuristic dreaming and strategic planning MUST have a strong relational element. I sum it up in my personal mission statement:

I merge my knowledge of being a futuristic and strategic thinker with the Relationship Building themes to help people plan and reach their potential.

Like every other tool listed in this chapter, the usefulness of the CliftonStrengths profile lies in its ability to help you determine your next steps. Use what you learn to decide what action steps to take on your goals, what books to read, and how you format your daily life. Use the knowledge gained to infuse power into your next steps. Don't let the results sit idly by in a file on your computer.

You'll learn more about how to incorporate these results into an action plan later on in this book, but focus on your strengths over weaknesses and you'll experience freedom from the pressure of performing at a less than optimal level.

4) The Enneagram Personality Test

As of the time of this writing, the Enneagram has experienced a surge of interest from those of all ages. It's the "in" test right now. You might have heard comments such as:

"Are you a 9!? I'm a 7 and proud of it."

"My mom's a 1. Now I know why she never let me help with the chores!"

"My boss is an 8. He can be rude, but man does he get things done!"

"My spouse is a 4; now I understand why they're so emotional."

That last one hits a little too close to home… My wife may not have said that last one out loud, but I bet she's thought it. I'm a 4 on the

Enneagram, so I can make fun of 4s. Each type has strengths and weaknesses. The beauty of the Enneagram is it exposes where we struggle and where we have the most problems.

Focusing on strengths is excellent, but to get to the core of who you are, to get to know the real you, it's important to recognize the areas where you struggle and will fall short. CliftonStrengths lifts you up, but the Enneagram slaps you in the soul. The power we have is learning to recognize ahead of time when life is getting ready to throw us a curveball so we can either adjust our swing or dive out of the way.

The Enneagram has nine main types, each with its own strengths and areas for growth. Below are some points on each to help you analyze your type. No person is likely to fit the type 100%, but you'll find you lean toward one or two.

One final caveat: As with the MBTI, there are ranges of maturity and development of each type. Mature 9s look almost completely different from developing 9s. This is the mistake people like Benjamin Hardy make when they say personality isn't permanent. Yes, we can and certainly should change and grow, but it doesn't mean our core selves are changing. It just means we are developing into the people we were meant to be.

Here are summary generalizations of the nine types, along with a few people who *might* align with the type):

1: The perfectionist (Harrison Ford, Julie Andrews, Eleanor Roosevelt)

- Patient and responsible
- Critical or judgmental
- Rule oriented
- Compares themselves to others

- Their word is everything
- Black-and-white worldview
- Produces monumental works when they finally finish
- Desires a life of service and integrity

2: The Helper (Glenn Close; Diana, Princess of Wales; Desmond Tutu)

- Takes care of others
- Thinks people should naturally understand other people's needs
- Great listener; empathetic
- Can spot the need in others
- Great at giving but struggle with receiving
- Sometimes give too much and expect the same back
- Has a hard time saying no
- Cares what people think

3: The Performer (Muhammad Ali, Lady GagGa, Will Smith)

- Competitive and loves to win
- Persuasive and cunning
- Go-getters
- Fast and furious
- Leaves others in the dust
- Leaders who struggle to follow
- Wins others over
- Workaholics

4: The Romantic (Cate Blanchett, Liam Neeson, Edgar Allan Poe)

- Dramatic
- Non-conformist
- Emotional

- Desires uniqueness and individuality
- Non-social but intense
- Sensitive and self-conscious
- Often misunderstood
- Extremely creative and attuned to the world's needs

5: The Investigator (Marie Curie, Bill Gates, Nikola Tesla)

- Takes care of self first
- Deeply analytical
- Puts thoughts over feelings to make decisions
- Prefers small groups over large crowds
- Can feel awkward around others
- Internal processors; need time to process what just happened

6: The Loyalist (Tom Hanks, Meg Ryan, Hugh Grant)

- Struggles with fear, anxiety, and the monster in the closet
- Strong observational skills
- Skeptical; likes to play devil's advocate
- Loyal, understanding, funny, and compassionate
- Has difficulty making decisions
- Productive and logical thinker

7: The Enthusiast (George Clooney, Whoopi Goldberg, Tina Turner)

- Full of life and energy
- Always ready for the next adventure
- More susceptible to addiction than other types
- Loves to keep options open
- Struggles to get important things done
- Gives others energy

8: The Challenger (Sandra Bullock, Winston Churchill, Frank Sinatra)

- Seeks justice and rightness
- Can be blunt, aggressive, and argumentative
- Stands up to bullies, usually not bullies themselves
- Loyal to a fault
- Tough exterior but are often passionate and sensitive underneath
- Leaders

9: The Peacemaker (Abraham Lincoln, Matt Damon, Queen Elizabeth II)

- Natural mediators who desire harmony
- Conflict avoidant
- Great followers and members of a team
- Non self-starting; thinks about themselves last
- Thrives with routine and organization
- Slow to start but hard to stop

The Enneagram highlights character flaws and strengths. Use it to understand your inner workings at a deeper level. If you don't agree with the findings, keep asking why to gain clarity.

5) Work History Test

This exercise comes from a book called *Will It Fly*[8] by entrepreneur and online business guru Pat Flynn. In the book, Pat lays out a series of exercises for testing out your next business idea. Before he dives into the business end, he starts with a series of tests designed to help

---

[8] Flynn, Pat. Will It Fly?: How to Test Your Next Business Idea So You Don't Waste Your Time and Money. e-book, Flynndustries, LLC, 2016.

the reader get to know themselves better.

The work history test may not sound riveting, but it helps to determine what kind of work you enjoy doing, which breeds growth and personal understanding. For your last three jobs, answer:

1. Job 1 Title:
2. What work did you do?
3. When? (timeframe)
4. What three things did you most enjoy?
5. What three did you least enjoy?
6. What is your favorite memory?
7. Final grade on a scale of A-D:

Here is an example of one of my past jobs so you can see how it's done.

What: Hawthorn Retirement Community Manager

When: November 2015- August 2017

What did you enjoy about it?

- *Marketing and learning new skills*
- *Building relationships with residents*
- *Proving that Miranda and I could work together*

What did you not enjoy about it?

- *Long hours and being on call*
- *Ridiculous levels of pressure to market and sell apartments above all else*
- *The day-to-day demands of having to cover jobs like serving, dishwashing, and cleaning*

What is your favorite memory?

- *Oak Park flapper party*
- *Miranda singing for our anniversary*
- *Our going away party from each building*

Grade: C

I found this exercise helpful for one specific reason: it highlighted how much I learned and grew from the experience. This is great for remembering that the things you are going through right now aren't forever but are molding you into the person you're becoming despite the pain and discomfort.

These tough times are shaping us into the stronger people we will eventually become. Use this test to understand the good and bad of past jobs to uncover hidden truths about your personality, strengths, and what you'd like to incorporate into your current work.

6) Determine Your Core Values

What matters most to you? What bothers you at a deep level? What makes you stand up on your soapbox? Core values aren't easy to determine, but knowing what you care about most is important as we continue to define the real you. Your values guide your actions, help you make big life decisions, and discover what matters most.

Values give meaning to our daily lives and help us set priorities. Values aren't selected; we discover and reveal them. If you start with a list, your conscious mind will test which values appear "better" than others. Instead, use the following thought experiment to determine your core values. Pick one word or phrase to describe your thoughts and experience in the following five scenarios. (I'll share my answers so you can see an example below):

1. Picture the most vivid or exciting memory you have of your adult life. What thoughts or feelings do you have about it?
2. Picture the last time you got into a heated discussion or debate. Why were you so riled up?
3. What is your strongest habit? Why?
4. Picture your perfect day. What kinds of things do you want to experience?
5. Lastly (and forgive the morbidity), what do you want them to say at your funeral? How would you end this sentence: (Your name) always lived with a passion and determination for _____

Using the above to determine my core values:

1. Hiking on Rigi Mountain in Switzerland. **Value: Freedom.**
2. A Heated discussion about people who live their lives in comfort and don't think outside the box. **Value: Non-Conformity.**
3. My strongest habit is doing something physically active every day: **Value: Wellbeing.**
4. My perfect day involves writing, spending time with Miranda, watching a Marvel movie, and eating a delicious meal. **Value: Family.**
5. Jordan always lived with a passion for helping people to achieve their dreams. **Value: Significance.**

What you care most about determines your energy for work and for continuing to pursue goals. Uncover your personal core values and continue to discover more about who you are. Exciting, isn't it? Even if you have an accurate sense of who you are and what you care about, sometimes just the act of writing it down unveils and counters previously mistaken assumptions.

7) Complete a Time Audit

Time is currency you can spend once. It doesn't rise or fall in value, we only become more aware of its passing as we age. A time audit will answer an important and potentially painful question; Does where you actually spend your time match with the core values you determined above? Do you spend enough time with family and friends, too much time working, or not enough time on your own personal growth?

Time is our greatest asset and the ultimate equalizer. We only have twenty-four hours to make the most of every day. Each day is an opportunity to choose how to spend the remaining hours of our lives. The important thing here is that you get to choose where you spend your time. Don't let your decisions default to how you feel in the moment or based upon what is expected of you. Go out and get *it*, whatever *it* is.

Time is a precious currency; how do you spend it? Not knowing why you do what you do is okay, but only for a time. Never settle for not knowing your why. I get to decide what to do with my life and where I put my time. It's a responsibility, but it's a choice, and one we all make whether we know it or not.

Record your answers to the time audit questions below:

1. What took up most of my time today? (Look at your calendar if needed or, gulp, your internet browser history).
2. What do I wish I did more of?
3. What did I do that I probably didn't need to do?
4. What's one thing I can do better tomorrow?

Based on the above, fill out what your ideal daily schedule would look like:

Time	Activity

Here is my ideal daily schedule:

Time	Activity
12:00 - 9:00	Sleep
9:00 - 10:00	Hour of power (reading, thinking, planning my day)
10:00 - 12:00	Breakfast, walk, starting work
12:00 - 5:00	Deep Work
5:00 - 5:30	Stretch/Meditate
5:30 - 7:00	Walk/run/exercise
7:00 - 8:00	Dinner
8:00 - 12:00 am	Free Time

8) Refresh Your Life Goals

My wife and I spent the lockdown/quarantine of 2020 in a small apartment in Lisbon, Portugal. It was exactly the type of place you'd want to be during such a time. Our landlord equipped it with all the essentials, it had an outdoor space to nab a few rays of sun, reliable Wi-Fi, and it felt like our own little private bubble.

As a solid introvert, I loved it. Being away from people for an extended period wasn't overly difficult, and the weather was perfect for walks, runs, and time outside. Overall, it was an enjoyable respite from the chaos of normal life.

The gentle breeze during a long walk, the post-run shot of endorphins, and the satisfaction of winning a game of Catan were priceless. It's weird to say I miss that time, but I really do. It was a time of rest and renewal, and I needed it. I'm happy to say I took advantage of the forced break to rest, recharge, and adjust my life goals. Oh, and I ran a half marathon. I did it because it felt good to have a big goal to reach for during an uncertain time.

I also played a ton of video games, read fiction novels, and ordered Uber Eats whenever the occasion called for it. It wasn't a perfect quarantine by any means. Having goals and marks to hit made it better than it could have been. Therefore, I'm convinced of the power of goals and always striving towards becoming better.

Setting goals and defining your life works wonders for discovering important facets of who you want to become. You can't know where you're going or even when you've arrived without a life compass. There are a ton of people feeling bad that they didn't make quarantine as successful as they could have. The same goes for anyone who can't reach a challenging New Year's resolution. Now that the world is moving forward and waking up, you might find that you didn't get as much done as you wanted to. So what?

There is no reason you can't start now and refresh your goals. Whenever I'm in a rut, I always find it valuable to reset and ask myself what I'm working toward, who I want to become, and what I want to accomplish. An energizing place to start is by completing the following life-goal refresh. Ask the following big life questions to get started:

- What are ten things I would like to accomplish? (Examples: Write twenty-five books, sell a business for $10 million, compete in a hot-pepper eating challenge and win.)
- What are ten things I would like to see? (Examples: The Pyramids, my daughter's wedding, the ocean from my screened-in porch.)
- What are ten things I would like to become? (Examples: An international speaker, a winner of the Nobel Peace Prize, a screenwriter for Disney/Pixar.)
- What are ten new things I could try? (Examples: Travel to outer space, cliff dive in Bermuda, win a poker tournament and qualify for the World Series of Poker.)
- What are ten things I would like to share with the world? (Examples: I want my children to have a love for reading, I want to become a local legend beekeeper and educate the public on the importance of bees, I want to direct an indie film picked up by Netflix.)

Get to fifty life goals and your eyes open up to the possibilities within your life. You'll see that life has so much more potential than you ever thought possible. I've spared you my list of goals here, but sign up for the free course for this book to access the example if you need further help.

Sometimes it's hard to start, but view this as a working list. It doesn't have to be complete or perfect. Make the goals as big or as small as you'd like. Breaking the goals down will come later on in this book when you formulate a 90-day plan.

**Do it with someone! Share this exercise with as many people as you'd like.*

9) The Two-Word Test

I first learned of the two-word test from the book *Younique: Designing the Life that God Dreamed for You*[9] by Will Mancini. The two-word exercise sheds light on the fact that you are probably living out a small part of your purpose right now, even if you don't know it. We all have something to contribute. This something exists as a small ember ready for you to coax into a burning flame.

The idea of the two-word test is to get to the core of what you want to do with your life based on what you are already good at. It takes these ideas and sums them up in two words. It will change over time as you get closer to your unique purpose, but for now develop something that fits your goals. I've adapted my version of the activity below. It has three parts you can complete in about 30 minutes:

1) Pick a signature scripture verse, famous quote, or movie line that best defines how you want to live your life.

2) Bullet journal 3-4 answers for each of these three questions:

- My strong abilities include...

---

[9] Mancini, Will. Younique: Designing the Life That God Dreamed for You. B&H Books, 2020.

- I have a deep passion for...
- I can use these abilities and passion in the context of...

3) Using the above as a guideline, pick two words that best describe your life mission. The first word ends in "ing," and the second word is a noun describing what you are changing. This is confusing, I know. Here are a few examples:

- "Encouraging Individuals"
- "Enlightening Truth"
- "Fostering Togetherness"
- "Establishing Peace"
- "Growing Teams"
- "Building Futures"
- "Coaching Growth"
- "Enabling Teens"
- "Winning People"
- "Engaging Hope"

Here is my two-word exercise so you can see how it works:

1) Signature phrase:

But be doers of the word, and not hearers only, deceiving yourselves. For if anyone is a hearer of the word and not a doer, he is like a man who looks intently at his natural face in a mirror. For he looks at himself and goes away and at once forgets what he was like. But the one who looks into the perfect law, the law of liberty, and perseveres, being no hearer who forgets but a doer who acts, he will be blessed in his doing." —James 1:22–25 (ESV)

2) Journal in bullet form:

My strong abilities include:

- Dreaming and leaning into the future
- Encouraging others
- Relating to people on different levels
- Sharing complex ideas in an easy-to-understand way
- Giving practical advice

I have a deep passion for:

- Seeing others succeed
- Taking action and gigantic risks
- Writing and creating useful content
- Enjoying and being engaged with work
- Strategy in life and in games

In the context of:

- The online world
- One-to-one coaching and conversations
- Writing books and updating my blog
- Videos and other content

3) Two-Word Phrase, Three Ideas:

- Encouraging Implementation
- Catalyzing Destiny
- Inspiring Boldness

Completing this exercise will go a long way toward increasing your self-awareness, and the ability to see and achieve what you want from your future. Remember, your two words will change over time and this is okay, but it's vital to consider future goals in the light of what you were born to do and who you want to become.

10) List Ten Things you Love About Yourself

This tool is the easiest one on the list. I've saved it for last because we are often our own worst enemies and biggest critics. We give ourselves so little credit and not enough grace. We deserve more than we give ourselves. We deserve to pat ourselves on the back with encouragement to keep going.

We will cover limiting beliefs later in this book, but this last tool will prime you for self-discovery and growth. Be honest with what you like about yourself and do the exercise now. Write out the ten traits about yourself you like most. If you need help, consider the following questions:

- What is a fun quality about myself I wouldn't want to lose?
- What quality about myself do I most admire?
- What is a time I did something heroic or brave?
- What is one trait I hope to pass on to a child, nephew, or mentee?

You are awesome. You have struggles, and no one is perfect, but take a few minutes to feel good about yourself with this tool before moving on to discovering your bigger Destiny.

Action Step: In my online course, The School of You, I share guided videos to walk you through all ten tools. Join the free companion course for this book first, and if you enjoy it, consider signing up for the School of You: https://www.jmring.com/cyd-book/

CHAPTER FOUR: BRINGING CLARITY TO DIFFERENCE

There's little to rival the exceptional experience of hiking Rigi Mountain in Switzerland. The crystal-clear water we crossed to get to the base, the tram ride along the mountainside, the breathtaking hike, the incredible views as far as the eye can see... There was nothing like it, and I'll be hard-pressed to experience something like it again. Until I go to the Moon, of course.

Up on that pristine mountain, Miranda and I realized something profound; it was something we knew about ourselves but not something each of us fully understood about the other person. We learned we experience the world in a substantially different way. On the mountain, Miranda was taking in the view, smelling the flowers, hearing the bleating of the mountain goats, and taking in every sight, smell, and sound. The feel of the grass and the slightly earthy taste brought to the lips by the mountain breeze rounded out her experience.

I was so entranced with deep thoughts about the world, what it means, and what could be that I hardly noticed any of those things. Hiking up the beautiful mountainside reinvigorated my zest and joy for life. It gave me energy for reaching my goals and for working toward my greater purpose. It filled me with the wonder of possibility and the soul-enriching power of nature at its finest.

On the MBTI Miranda is an ISFJ and I'm an INFJ. We differ on the N and the S, and we never felt it as strongly as when we were on

Rigi mountain. It brought our differences out into the light. But instead of confusion or chaos, we took the time to communicate our experiences. It became a shared experience we will never forget. She gave me insights into her experience, and I shared mine with her.

One mountain. Two people. Two very different experiences. One moment of intense understanding.

Labels: Dangerous or Helpful?

People are different. Duh, right? All it takes is a stroll down a busy sidewalk, a game night with friends, or a family reunion to see this plain as day. The problem is some of the biggest misunderstandings take place when and where people are different. Understanding gives us clarity and insight into human behavior and leads to a better world, where people not only survive their differences, they thrive.

I know people who avoid labels at all costs. You might be in such a group. I get it. No one likes being put in a box. What I'm espousing in this book is worth the risk. It's understanding yourself and others at the cost of identifying with certain traits and characteristics. It's looking at commonalities among people and behaviors to understand why we act the way we do.

The insights we've gained from self-discovery are worth the risk. Joking with Miranda and saying, "That's your 9 coming out!" Or "You're using your S really hard right now, I'm not tracking with you at all," has given us the ability to communicate at a higher level than we ever thought possible. Never use personality tests to excuse behavior, but to understand and grow.

Many people use these labels and insights in the wrong way. Believing something like "Well, Jordan's an INFJ, so he doesn't care what others think," is not only false, but dangerous. INFJs are typically deeply caring and principled individuals, who sometimes have a hard time showing how much they care.

Labels can be dangerous, but only in the wrong hands. In our hands, we'll use labels for understanding and communicating. Insights gained from self-discovery and reflection are invaluable for personal growth. Always compare new lessons with prior knowledge and use additional information to beget further understanding.

Discovering Patterns and Tendencies

No one agrees on who said this originally, but at various times it's been attributed to Albert Ellis, Walter Michel, B.F. Skinner, and Mark Twain:

"The best predictor of future behavior is past behavior."

This may be true in general, but it doesn't have to be true for you. You have the power to rise above your patterns and delve into a new future. That's the purpose of this book! But the starting point is discovering patterns and tendencies. Begin with the end goal in mind to discover patterns and tendencies. It's why you gain the most from taking several approaches to determining who you are. As I've said before, no one test can or will define you. You're a unique individual with a special purpose. But understanding your bigger life purpose begins with self-discovery.

Knowing how you acted in the past can prevent you from acting like that in the future. If I know I have difficulty experiencing the moment (which I do) I'll learn to breathe deep, take in the sights and sounds, and experience the moment for what it is. I can still be me and experience something deeply, but also appreciate the moment.

We can choose a better tomorrow. We can (and should!) embrace who we are and be proud of it. But this doesn't mean we need to suffer from our shortcomings and lagging issues.

You and I will always have certain tendencies. We will always lean a certain way. Embracing who we are and loving ourselves means that this is okay. We don't have to be something we are not. There is much freedom in this. Personality isn't permanent, but we are different. You absolutely have the power to change and rise above:

- Anyone can be a public speaker, regardless of their level of introversion.
- Anyone can be a dreamer, even if they are more practical and observant.
- Anyone can learn to show more empathy, even if it's unnatural at first.
- Anyone can become a go-getter, regardless of their tendency to keep their options open.

Growth is possible for anyone. You have the power and capability to rise above your current preset of characteristics and become who you want to be. Personality isn't a label, it doesn't put you in a box, nor is it permanent. Self-discovery is all about unearthing patterns and tendencies and then pushing forward with what you know to be true about you.

Can I Do Anything?

You can do anything you set your mind to. But this is the answer to the wrong question. The better question is, should you do it?

In the movie *Jurassic Park*, one of the main characters, Ian Malcolm, says:

"Your scientists were so preoccupied with whether they could, they didn't stop to think if they should…"

I believe I could become an extrovert who only makes decisions with logic and analytics. I could become this type of person. But to do so would deny who I am! The right path is becoming who we were born to be, not just something you want to be or think you should be. You have a specific purpose. You differ from other people. Life still isn't easy, but it becomes a heck of a lot more enjoyable. Work doesn't seem like work. You need only merge your deepest desires with your passions and personality, and voila, the curtain gets swept aside, and your purpose revealed through your identity.

You can do anything you set your mind to, but you shouldn't. Instead, find out what you were meant to do, embrace who you were born to be, and focus on your strengths.

Action step: How could a renewed understanding of personalities affect your ability to get along with troublesome people? Write the name of a difficult person below along with a few ideas of what you could do to overcome.

_____

_____

_____

CHAPTER FIVE: MISSION POSSIBLE

The retirement community where Miranda and I were assistant community managers was at 63% capacity, and this needed to change. The goal of 80% by the end of three months was set, the game was afoot, and the pressure was on. I've never liked pressure of any kind and felt the pounding in my heart. Was I ready for this? It was like game seven of the world series, except the closest we got to this level of competition was balloon volleyball in the atrium.

"How many prospects do we have on the horizon, Jordan?" My boss Jim asked with a touch of impatience on a busy Monday morning.

With the phone clutched to my face like a jacket on a chilly day, I responded nervously, "We have a few tours scheduled, and another couple who's coming in again this Friday to see apartment 234. We're working our hardest over here."

"Well, you know what you need to do," He said as he ended our brief conversation.

Gulp. We needed to sell more apartments. Fast. I actually liked my boss a lot. He was gracious, kind, and trustworthy, but he had bosses too. Our deadline was approaching, and things didn't look good. I needed to figure out what the heck I was doing. We all did. The building couldn't stay open at 63% capacity. We were leaking money.

You know the old maxim, "fake it 'til you make it?" Well, it doesn't work when you're trying to get people to uproot themselves from the comfort of their home, put their trust in you, and hand you a check. It's a tad bit more complicated. But all challenging and worthwhile endeavors are.

Miranda believed in me, of course, but as the marketing lead in our husband-and-wife duo, it was my responsibility to get people to move in. We were at an old building, out in the middle of nowhere, and there was no urgency to fill the place (other than from upper management), so this was no small task. This retirement community building was beautiful, with fantastic views of the golden countryside, luxury apartments, and exquisite food prepared by a team of chefs. So what the heck was the problem?

You could tout many reasons, all of which were true: the management turnover was high, the location was quite remote, and most of the local clientele couldn't afford our prices. But the only reason that mattered was that the building had never been filled, and thus, no one thought it was possible. It's probably why they sent Miranda and me to the building. We had little clue what we were doing, but maybe, just maybe, we'd be naïve enough to believe we could do it. We knew nothing, but someone higher up knew what they were doing by sending us there.

One month in, our other management team quit, leaving us with one training manager. Three weeks later she left in the middle of the night without so much as a goodbye. Two days later, our regional manager quit too. Suddenly, the entire weight of the building was on our shoulders and the head of the company had to meet with us to make a plan (and to ensure that we were, in fact, not going to up and leave as well). Two brand-new managers who were just a couple of kids leading the place... Crazy, right? Wrong. You do what you have to do. You rise to the challenge. You embrace the suck and make the best of whatever situation you find yourself in.

We took our learning in stride, even with the many challenges and difficulties. I'd never cried as often, and I haven't cried as much since. Being in that building was one of the hardest things I've ever done. Between late-night emergency calls, shifting managers, operational struggles, and impossible marketing goals, it's a wonder we stayed sane.

But we fought through. We upped our resiliency meter tenfold. I can honestly say I'm glad for the growth we experienced because of our efforts. We joke that the stress took years off our lives, and it probably did, but it helped shape me into someone who doesn't quit and never says never. I don't take no for an answer, and it's because I pushed through.

I don't know when it happened, but we started believing it was possible to fill the building. Maybe we started drinking the company Kool-Aid? Whatever the reason, we hit a renewed sense of Destiny as Miranda kept the building operational with her organizational expertise, and I finally started selling apartments. It was the belief in the possible that fueled our efforts, and we finally gained momentum. I was selling rooms left and right!

I used to be in awe of our training manager, who could meet potential residents for a tour, and by the end of the thirty minutes would wave a deposit check in a not-so-humble brag. This brief fascination ended during one particular weekly check- in call during the summer of 2016.

"Jordan, are we still looking at one move-in this week?" Jim said on the call.

"Hey Jim, sorry for the change, but we're looking at three now." I said with unrestrained excitement in my voice.

The surprise on the other end was golden. Here we were, the building that was ALWAYS last in the company, throwing in a surprise two move-ins at the last minute to continue our latest dominance.

"Did you say three, Jordan? Repeat that please." he said, his voice tripping slightly.

Never had our building had as much momentum. We had just passed the building's record occupancy of 83% and were showing no signs of slowing down. Not to be too on the nose with the lesson, but we only did it because we believed we could. If you believe you can, you will. No goal is impossible if pursued relentlessly. The relentless pursuit of a goal is all you need to achieve it. Sometimes the best path to victory is a commitment to see things through.

The solution isn't elegant or sexy. Unfortunately, hard work, determination, and the belief that your goal is reachable is all you need. As soon as you think you can't, you can't. As soon as you think you can, you're one step closer to Destiny.

Every person has limiting beliefs that affect their lives. Does this sound like you? It sounds like me. Entire companies suffer from the pervasiveness of negative beliefs. What are your limiting beliefs? What do you believe about your current situation, circumstance, or skills you are letting hold you back? What is stopping you from becoming a better version of yourself?

Luckily, the more you grow in self-awareness, the less limiting beliefs will restrain your progress. We move beyond what we think we can do into the realm of possibility. We become possibilists.

Living out The Possible

We still have some self-discovery work to do. Nothing in the rest of this book will matter an iota if you don't first believe you can do great things and change the world for the better. And I know, saying "you can do it, champ!" won't help. It doesn't matter if I or anyone else thinks you can do it, it matters if *you* think you can. It's an important distinction.

Thomas Edison once said:

"If we all did the things we are capable of doing, we would literally astound ourselves."

Impossible tasks don't exist, only small minds. Do you believe you are capable of astounding yourself? You probably are, but you might not know it or believe it. I was capable of selling apartments, but it wasn't until I looked past my self-doubt and personal reservations that I succeeded. I breathed in the possible and went for it. I dug in, learned what I could, made a ton of mistakes, and continued to reiterate until I started getting checks.

We all have limitations. Our circumstances might prevent us from achieving what we most desire. You aren't stuck in your current circumstance. This is a myth. No life circumstance is forever unless you believe it to be so. Contrary to popular belief, there is never a point in which we are permanently stuck.

To live out what's possible and discover a deeper purpose, believe it's possible for you. To Catalyze Your Destiny, believe you have a Destiny to Catalyze. You're interested in your purpose and life goals, so I won't belabor the point. There's a straightforward test to see if you believe you have a unique purpose and Destiny to fulfill. The answer to this question determines if you have limiting beliefs that are holding you back.

Are you actively pursuing your passion and purpose?

That's it. Are you actively pushing forward and investing in your life? Or are you sitting on the sidelines, waiting for life to happen to you and playing if "safe?"

Reading this book doesn't count as an action step. As much as you love books and find them absolutely necessary for personal growth, don't take the easy path. Try (and maybe fail) to sell apartments. Cook the new healthy recipe. Enroll in a local dance class to rekindle the fire with your significant other. Don't sit on the sidelines. Just get going.

It's too early in the book to hop up on my action soapbox, but there is no better way to learn than by doing. I failed so many times to sell apartments until I didn't. My learning could have been propelled with a great marketing book (and I read several), but I still had to do the work and sell. Nothing beats experience.

Keeping your options open is fantastic, and learning more is helpful, but you have to eventually take the plunge and take action on what you learned. A healthy balance between planning and taking action is key. Gaining confidence in who you are and living out what's possible depends on finding the right mix for your specific situation.

Are you ready to become a possibilist? Are you ready to embrace the fact that you are amazing and have incredible potential? Your road to self-discovery is incomplete without it. Purpose is meaningless without its power. Your 90-day plan will implode before the first day if you don't embrace the possible. If you are ready to take a chance on yourself, put on your best set of shoes and start walking towards purpose.

Action Step: Take a small action step towards self-discovery and growth by seizing the day and making it extraordinary. Don't settle for less by thinking you aren't capable of reaching great heights.

CHAPTER SIX: THE FIRE BURNING WITHIN

Ruth was a charming soul. She would always smile and greet you. She was quiet and unassuming, but you could tell she had lived a full and happy life. I only knew her briefly, but I'll never forget finding her in her final peaceful slumber, having breathed her last in her small but lovely apartment. Her memory will always live on with me and others who knew her best.

It was all about the people.

Living and working in the retirement community brought sadness and joy. Sadness in the moments of pain, loss, and suffering; joy in getting to know wonderful people. It was such an up-and-down time for us: Walking into an apartment only to discover that a resident you loved had died in their sleep. Continuing to serve the remaining residents, seeing a smile on their faces when you made the coffee rounds at dinner, but feeling the weight of the world on your shoulders. The time passed rapidly and yet agonizingly slowly. I'm thrilled I'm past that season of my life, but I miss the people. I miss the joy. I miss the moments where one smile changed someone's day. I miss the personal impact I had.

One thing I don't miss? The ugly stench of regret that permeated the lives of far too many residents. Too much regret, sadness, and shame. Unless you've worked in this kind of environment, it's hard to communicate what it feels like. It was present on too many faces. The people believed they were done and had arrived at their final act. For some, this was true, as they only had a few months to live. For most, regret was all too present, all too early. I don't care if you're 7 or 77; you have much left to give! A select few reveled in the chance to make their last days extraordinary. It's the legacy of these fine folks I hope to pass on.

This longing for others to live out their purpose has been a fire inside my soul ever since I was young, but I never noticed how much it got to me until seeing the seniors' faces, old, tired, and full of regret. It saddens me to this day, but it instilled in me the zeal to write, to create, and to make a difference. It emboldened me to make the most of every day.

This thing I can't stand, this regret, has become the fuel for the fire of my life purpose. In two words, my purpose mirrors the title of this book, to Catalyze Destiny. I want to show people how to live without regret through self-discovery and personal growth. It's my purpose to launch you toward a life lived without regret.

What Is the One Thing You Can't Stand?

What lights a fire in your eyes when you talk about it? What gets your engine going? What infuriates you?

In this closing chapter in the first section, before we dive into life purpose, we'll look at what bothers you the most. This is unique to you and not something derived from your parents, church, best friend, or boss. Put a name on what ignites the fires of your heart, and you'll define your unique purpose. Channel your energy for changing something important, merge this with your individual skills and strengths, and you have a winning recipe for success.

You can't channel every dislike or preference into purpose. An anti-cats campaign wouldn't go too far even though I can't stand those little feline devils (if you love cats, bless you, but please keep them away from me). Not everything you dislike should turn into your purpose. It doesn't matter how much I dislike cats, I won't make it my life's purpose to eradicate the world of cats. Other people find love and contentment from animals, and I would never take that away from them. I would also never go against someone pushing for animal rights, as long as they don't ask me to hold Garfield or Spot while they picket.

What you can't stand might relate to a hot-button issue involving politics, religion, or global relations. It's not just something you don't like, it's a value you want to see changed. It's an unfair act. It's something that is but shouldn't be. It's the one thing, above all others, that ignites a fire within your soul.

A few examples:

- You can't stand the urge to have a busy lifestyle. **Purpose**: Educate people on the benefits of living life slowly with a minimalistic attitude.
- You can't stand stereotypes and unfair judgement. **Purpose**: Encourage those who believe in freedom and change hearts and minds.
- You can't stand obesity. **Purpose**: You become a health nut whose energy is infectious and you help people make better life decisions.
- You can't stand war and fighting: **Purpose**: You develop solutions for conflict management and building better teams.
- You can't stand division. **Purpose**: You bridge the gap through peaceful conversations, learning on each side, and encourage better plans that work for everyone.

- You can't stand divorce or relational struggle. **Purpose**: Counsel couples to grow closer together and develop strategies for better communication.

This list could go on and on, but you get the idea. You could fight everything you can't stand, but I urge you to focus on only one problem. Try to do too much and you end up doing nothing. Try to change what isn't yours to change and you'll end up spinning your wheels.

In his book *The One Thing*,[10] Gary Keller writes:

"Success demands singleness of purpose. You need to be doing fewer things for more effect instead of doing more things with side effects. It is those who concentrate on but one thing at a time who advance in this world."

If you want to change the thing you can't stand, make it the single drive for your purpose. There are far too many problems and not enough people directly trying to solve those problems. We can't change everything, and we shouldn't try. Our ability to affect change is finite. Use the resources you have while you have them.

If everyone knew themselves better, picked a lane of purpose, stayed in that lane, and made reachable and powerful goals, the world would become infinitely better. It's a lofty goal and ideal, I know. But the power of seeding your purpose with your heart's desire for change is real and tangible. You need only to reach out and grab yours.

---

[10] Keller, Gary, and Jay Papasan. The ONE Thing: The Surprisingly Simple Truth Behind Extraordinary Results. Illustrated, e-book, Bard Press, 2013.

The Seed of Your Purpose: Solving the Problem

The good news? Focusing on a single problem means letting go of the guilt of other burdens. There are other causes I *could* help and make a difference for, but I ask myself: is my energy best suited for this area or another? Where can I make the most difference and impact? Be a part of your best-fit solution and nothing else. This mindset frees you from the weight of hoisting all the world's problems on your shoulders. It's a breath of fresh air for anyone who so desperately needs oxygen.

Homelessness bothers me. Abortion is wrong. And while cancel culture is slowly making its way up the list of things I can't stand, I'm staying in my lane.

Every time I think, "Man, I just need to write a Facebook post to tell the world how strongly I feel about the above topics…" I force myself to say, "No, that doesn't fit with MY purpose. It's a distraction from changing the world in the way I'm meant to change it. It might bother me, but it doesn't ignite a true fire in my soul like the dangers of regret and passive living.

And while I'm certainly entitled to my opinion on the above, opinions don't change the world. Action does. But action costs time, and we only have so much of this valuable resource. We must spend it wisely.

One pain point + one purpose = maximum output. The formula isn't complicated. All you need do is unleash the aching of your heart into an outpouring of solid action. What you can't stand comprises unequal parts:

- Past trauma (parents divorcing, abuse, hardship in school, unbalanced negative criticism, etc.).

- What makes your blood boil right now.
- What bothers you most about yourself or others.
- What you believe you can change.

Fueling purpose with what bothers you most is exciting, isn't it? It's a chance for you to make something out of your life and unleash the desires of your heart. I hope you sense and feel my love for this topic. As the words make their way from my brain to my fingers and to the keyboard, I'm virtually shouting with excitement for you to experience an infusion of hope.

Your unique purpose is tied to what you can't stand the most. We could almost end the book here (except that it's always more complicated than that, and I don't want to leave you hanging), but the story doesn't end here. It starts when you take ownership for changing what you can't stand the most. It ends only when your legacy fades into nothingness, years and years beyond your lifespan.

Once you name your life purpose and discover how to make it a reality, you can change the world for the better. Not only will it make each one of your days ahead better, but you'll also no longer live with regret… How could you? If you live every day with an effort to deepen the effectiveness of your purpose, you won't have time to feel sorry. If every day is a win, you'll live the rest of your days in the absolute sureness of meeting your potential. And that's a grand place to be.

Action Step: Write down or say aloud your answers to the following questions to spark your purpose fire:

1.   *What's an event you could use to fuel future change?*
2.   *What makes your blood boil?*
3.   *What's something you wish you could change about yourself or someone else?*
4.   *What's something you believe doesn't have to be?*

*Expressing your thoughts brings clarity. **You don't need to develop a plan right now, just start thinking about what you can't stand.***

PART TWO:

REVEAL YOUR PURPOSE WITH THE
FOUR POINTS OF PURPOSE OF THE IKIGAI

CHAPTER SEVEN: DISCOVER THE FOUR POINTS OF PURPOSE WITH THE IKIGAI

I love the Moon...

It's an iridescent pearl shining in the night. It's there by day, unassuming and popping up all over the place. It's a constant reminder that wherever we are on the planet, we are connected by something eternally small in the universe, but massive to our eyes and emotions. But we aren't small. We're large and in charge, no matter our physical size. I love this quote from Neil deGrasse Tyson:

Ever look up at the night and feel small? Don't. Instead, feel large. Atoms in our bodies trace to the remnants of exploded stars. We are stardust. We are alive in the universe. And the universe is alive within us.

I love the thought of being stardust. It infuses me with power in mind and body. How does it make you feel? Maybe not a lot different? Maybe it makes you feel powerful.

It's worth remembering our part in the cosmic play of life. Determining what part we'll play is the goal of the second section in this book and, ultimately, your life. It starts with the age-old question, the one we've all asked while staring up at the night sky and the brilliant Moon...

What am I here for?

The meaning of life... The big question many of us ask at various milestones. Most of us consider this grand question when it's too late, ignoring what's most important because life is busy and too demanding. I've been there. I get it. It's not easy. Yet you will, at some point or another, consider this ultimate of questions. It's critical to ask before it's too late. Jump on the fast track now by determining your purpose.

There is no greater way to sum up the desperate search for purpose than these words by the late Chadwick Boseman,[11] the one and only Black Panther, to the graduating class of Howard University in Washington, D.C.:

> *Graduating class, hear me well on this day; this day, when you have reached the hilltop, and you are deciding on next jobs, next steps, careers, further education: You would rather find purpose than a job or a career.*

> *Purpose crosses disciplines. Purpose is an essential element of you. It is the reason you are on the planet at this particular time in history. Your very existence is wrapped up in the things you are here to fulfill. Whatever you choose for a career path, remember, the struggles along the way are only meant to shape you for your purpose.*

> *When I dared to challenge the system that would relegate us to victims and stereotypes with no clear historical backgrounds, no hopes or talent, when I questioned that method of portrayal, a different path opened up for me, the path to my Destiny. When God has something for you, it doesn't matter who stands against it.*

---

[11] "Remembering Actor Chadwick Boseman." NPR, https://www.npr.org/2020/08/29/907512165/remembering-actor-chadwick-boseman. Accessed 27 Dec. 2020.

Finding life purpose is challenging. You know that. Unless you're already knee-deep in your purpose and know exactly what you need to do every day, you're still in painful discovery mode. A powerful way of determining purpose and surviving the painful process of discovery is by using a tool called the Ikigai ("ik-ee-guy"). This Japanese word means "reason for being." We will use it in this section as a starting point and as a tool for determining purpose. It's a way of thinking and being that will bring meaning, contentment, and lasting fulfilment to your life.

The only problem with the Ikigai? It's difficult to use it unless you back it with self-knowledge and personal understanding. It's akin to going apple picking with an eagerness to find the juiciest apples, but Dad didn't do his research, and the apple orchard is closed because of COVID-19. Good one, Dad.

The Ikigai loses its efficacy (and becomes pointless) if the orchard is closed and you don't have apples to pick. Knowing more about yourself is the first step. Using the Ikigai is the second. And taking action is the last part. But since you did the work in the first section (right?) you're ready to go! The Ikigai is made up of four parts. Everything you do, every activity or task, will fall somewhere on the continuum. It's best pictured as a Venn diagram:

The Ikigai and the Four Points of Purpose

A Japanese Approach to Discovering Life Purpose

Feeling of uselessness. Work doesn't matter.

Lacking financial security. Unsustainable contentment.

What You **Love**

Happy and Productive

Happy and Influential

What You Are **Good** At

Ikigai!

What the World **Needs**

Financial Security and Productive

Influential and Financial Security

What You Can Get **Paid** For

Comfortable with status quo. Not passionate about work.

Lacking skills. Confusion at progress and narrowing of options.

The four parts of your Ikigai are:

1. What you love to do
2. What the world needs
3. What you're actually good at
4. What you can get paid for

The bottom line? When what you do fills you with passion and contentment, is something the world desperately needs, you're great at it (or can learn to get better), and you can get paid to do it, you will fulfil your true purpose. This simplified approach to the nebulous and individualistic topic of purpose isn't perfect, but it's a beginning. It's a way for you to develop your unique potential. It's how you can use your skills, strengths, and tendencies to make a lasting impact and enjoy life.

The balance between the four points of purpose isn't sexy, but it's key to defining your mission in life. There is no one-size-fits-all answer, but with careful reflection and implementation of the four points, you'll get closer. You'll never be in perfect harmony all the time, and that's okay. There will be times you don't love what you do, your bank account is empty, your skills don't perfectly match your activity, and you're burnt out from giving back and need a break. We will all go through varying degrees of misalignment. I've been there more than I would like to admit.

You'll find true purpose with a mix of the four points. The combination is unique to you. It's slow to develop and even changes with time. Reaching for perfection is not the goal (I can see you Enneagram ones freaking out right about now). You do NOT have to hit the height of each point to have purpose, but reaching for it is still your best bet.

You could find a purpose that fills the first three but doesn't make any money. Maybe someone could bankroll you while you get started? Maybe you hate what you do, but the world needs it, you are the expert in it, and it's raking in the dough? Maybe you're willing to make that sacrifice in the short term? Transitions are temporary, but life is one big transition. We are growing and changing all the time. If you reach three out of the four points of purpose, good for you, but you won't reach your Ikigai, nor will life be as fulfilling as it could be.

Ultimately, you must have a foot in the door on each point. The four points of purpose are equal, and each demands your attention. Not loving what you do will eventually lead to burnout. Not doing something the world needs will end in selfish gain that isn't fulfilling. Not doing something you're good at is a waste of time and resources you could spend doing what you were born to do. Not getting paid will eventually lead to anger, resentment, or the obvious but unacceptable consequence of financial instability. Three out of four isn't good enough, and won't lead to lasting fulfilment.

You won't always love what you do, and not everything you do contributes to greater meaning, but each is crucial for long-term contentment and fulfilling your Destiny. You don't need to determine your number-one goal right this second, but take steps to figure it out. Seeking purpose grants meaning and lifts you up toward your Destiny. Have an eye for these four points and use them as a lens for future decisions. This section is here to bring greater awareness to what you're already doing and give you clarity and energy to take the next step.

John C. Maxwell, international speaker, leadership guru, and one of my favorite authors, says:

"The two greatest days of your life are the day you were born and the day you find out why."

If you know your purpose, if you work every day on your number-one desire and goal, you'll build unstoppable momentum in your life. Over the past five years, my purpose has crystalized. I still feel like I've only uncovered 10% of my purpose, and I have tons of room for growth and development, but I'm continuing to figure it out day by day. I'm working on what I do best and will figure out everything else as I go.

Get busy figuring out what your purpose is, or get busy living it. Read the rest of this book, read other books, try new things, ask others for feedback. If you know what you're supposed to do, what's impeding the next step? The absolute worst place to be is "I'll do it someday..." DON'T get stuck here. Move forward with what you know and take action. In the following purpose driven chapters, we'll cover each of the four points of purpose as diagrammed by the Ikigai. At the end of this section, I'll prompt you to fill out one for yourself.

Action Step: Name your purpose out loud or write it down. There's power in naming your current purpose in writing or by speaking it aloud to a friend. Even if your current purpose is to find your ultimate purpose, that's okay! Your purpose can (and probably will) change. I encourage this.

CHAPTER EIGHT: HOW DO I FIND MY PASSION?

In high school, I always arrived bright and early to complete my homework. In a few classes I merely existed; in most I thrived. Tennis and band practice kept me busy after school. I was home to eat at 5:30. I played Halo 2 in the evenings. I worked at a grocery store on the weekends. Eat, sleep, repeat.

I miss the simple, predictable, and mostly enjoyable high school life. I didn't have to make many life-altering decisions, and I had a more consistent daily and weekly routine than at any point in my life since. I view this time with rose-colored glasses, of course. It was also the time when the school bullies picked me as their target, I was lacking in confidence, and I was deathly afraid of talking to pretty girls. I'm glad I didn't meet Miranda back then, I might never have talked to her!

I played the trumpet, served aces on the tennis court, and dominated noobs in Halo 2. My activities didn't vary all that much, but I enjoyed them. I was a nerdy kid with only a few hobbies. Though I grew up in Maine, I never went snowboarding, didn't eat lobster, and rarely enjoyed the outdoors other than to play airsoft with some buddies in the woods. I wasn't all that cool or popular, but I was okay with it.

I wouldn't trade my upbringing and experiences for anything. Everything we go through is part of who we are. Everything we've ever enjoyed doing is part of our mold. We are the sum of all of our parts, and the things we love are a huge part of this. I may not play as much tennis as I used to, but I'm still a tennis player. These experiences are part of my identity.

You probably don't have one singular passion. I sure don't. This is normal. And just like people, passion comes in various shapes and sizes. Your love for swimming might not rival Michael Phelps' passion for the sport, and this is okay. You don't have to name swimming as your-number one passion and then figure out how to make it work for your career.

Passions change, and such is the danger of focusing only on what you're passionate about. My passions have developed into reading, travelling, writing, and exploring the world with my wife. I appreciate the power of getting outside my comfort zone, and even though I'm never thrilled with a big change, I embrace it wholeheartedly.

Some people are more passionate than others. I have friends who love to try new things and dive in with both feet at every new opportunity life throws at them. I'm not like that. I've only had a few activities I would consider passions. While I hope to one day get more into oil painting, archery, and biking, I can count on one hand the things I'm truly passionate about. This dialed-in focus is especially useful when reaching for a big goal like writing a book, but we don't know what we don't know. How do I know I don't love to ski, bungee jump, or speak Mandarin? How do I know I don't love caving, fencing, or soap carving?

You don't know what you don't know. There is more out there than we realize and I implore you to try new things. It's age-old wisdom, but it's worth adding here. We all need to be trying new things as often as we can. I've become more of a risk-taker these last few years, and it's paid off in my personal growth and journey.

The advice of "follow your passion" is good, but it's incomplete. We are better off if we enjoy what we do, but we need to be clear on what this means in practice by thinking about how this topic relates to the other three points of purpose. If you have a passion in mind for your Ikigai, run it through these three questions:

1. Does this specific passion help others significantly? If not, what outside-the-box ideas might make it work?
2. Am I passionate enough about the activity that I could turn it into my number-one paying gig?
3. Do I have the time and the talent to get great at it?

Passion isn't hiding from the world or playing video games non-stop. It might feel good for the short term, but it doesn't lead to fulfilment. Passion that leads to fulfilment for yourself and others is what we are after. If you're creative enough, anything can work. I could envision a high school tennis boot camp that teaches strong morals or a writing club gathering together to work on their life-changing manuscripts. I don't want to do those things, but someone could. Exercising your Ikigai muscle forces you to ask several layers of questions for your idea.

Seeking my Ikigai, the intersection of the four points of purpose, doesn't mean I can't bake bread on the side as a hobby, it just means it won't be my number-one goal and focus. This is of the utmost importance for later on, as you strive to take action and work on determining your purpose. Life will throw so much at you, but if you know your number-one desire and focus, you are primed to make time for it.

Eventually, you'll find that you do less and less of the tasks and hobbies that don't relate to your purpose. You'll still be able to have a barbecue with friends or spend the day at the beach, but once your focus becomes clear, and you know what you're here to do, it's hard to stop doing it. We don't know the world's biggest influencers for their hobbies or what they did in their spare time. We know them for how they fueled their purpose by living out passionate and focused lives.

Some people might never know true happiness, which sucks, but this is why people just like you are reading this book. If we can interlock purposes and spread love, joy, and unbridled happiness, the world can and will be changed. This is my purpose. This is what my completed Ikigai looks like. I'd love for you to know yours and know where you want to go.

Every life changed fuels my passion to keep writing and creating content. We've come far as a species. We still have a long way to go. But it's time we all started doing what we are most passionate about and finding joy and contentment with our lives.

What is Passion?

Terms are often thrown about willy-nilly when talking about passion and doing what you love. We won't do that here. We'll come up with our own definition. But first, Webster's definition[12] of passion:

"A strong feeling of enthusiasm or excitement for something or about doing something."

Our enhanced definition for this book:

"A deep contentment that comes from repeatedly doing something you love with others."

---

[12] "Passion." The Merriam-Webster.Com Dictionary, 18 Dec. 2020, www.merriam-webster.com/dictionary/passion.

Following your passion doesn't mean just enjoying a solo day out on the waves. It means sharing your passion with others by teaching surfing to kids, making how-to YouTube videos, or creating an online surfing course. To turn something you like into a passion, it needs to lead somewhere beyond just a day of fun for you. The waves of passion need to expand beyond you into other people's lives.

Following your passion means doing what you love as part of the four points of purpose. It has to involve other people, or it won't work long term. But it starts with knowing what you like and powering through where you are right now.

Not Following Your Passion

Passion doesn't need to fill you with intense pleasure every time you do it. In fact, you can find passion and joy in doing deep, quality, and fervent work for focused periods of time. This is especially true if you're already talented in what you do.

Cal Newport, in his book *So Good They Can't Ignore You*[13] says:

"Passion comes after you put in the hard work to become excellent at something valuable, not before. In other words, what you do for a living is much less important than how you do it."

Cal Newport is offering the opinion that how you do something matters more than what you do. He believes talent and skill trump passion because enjoyment comes from being valued and empowered by a job well done.

He also shares:

---

[13] Newport, Cal. So Good They Can't Ignore You: Why Skills Trump Passion in the Quest for Work You Love. e-book, Grand Central Publishing, 2012.

"The happiest, most passionate employees are not those who followed their passion into a position, but instead those who have been around long enough to become good at what they do. On reflection, this makes sense."

Newport suggests leading with skills and focusing on getting better at whatever you are doing to find passion. He believes hard work and development of high levels of talent create a passion for the task itself, and thus you can find joy and contentment with any job.

This is one option. It might work for you. But it's not the only option.

Myth: Someone Has to Do It

My problem with Newport's approach is that it doesn't make sense for everyone. It only works as an augmentation, not as a starting point. No matter how good you get at a certain job or task, you'll never find genuine passion and happiness if you're not in the right environment or fit. This applies to work, home environment, where you live, who you associate with, etc.

An Enneagram one (the perfectionist) will never enjoy a job focused more on quick results than quality work. An ISFJ (Myers-Briggs) will struggle to work as a head chef in a busy and demanding restaurant. A person with Ideation as their number-one CliftonStrength will feel suffocated in an environment steeped in tradition and sameness.

My first job was at a grocery store in my small hometown in Maine. As a fifteen-year-old kid, I stocked shelves full of milk, soda pop, and baking supplies; wrapped and priced rib eyes and ground chuck; and eventually worked the registers as a clerk. To say the work quickly became dull and monotonous would be an understatement. It was quite dreadful, and the hours passed painfully slowly. My future wasn't there.

Today, I have massive respect for retail workers, cashiers, and front-line workers who served during the COVID-19 crisis and continue to get up every day to serve their communities. But most would probably choose to be anywhere else during this time. Very few people would choose to be behind a register wearing a mask 40+ hours per week just to pay the bills. This isn't happiness and passion.

Maybe you feel different. Maybe you believe the myth that "someone has to do it." But this shortsighted line of thinking reduces individual potential, and worse, gives you an out for pursuing a job way below your skills and abilities. Most in-person services will be conducted online in the near future. It's already happening with the rise of Amazon and other online shopping portals. Like it or not, things are changing and the adaptable will thrive.

My point is simple: you can't find passion in just anything you do. We are meant for more. You are meant for more. Our super-powered brains crave deep work, challenging problems, and giving back in meaningful and lasting ways. Give your brain what it needs. Don't settle for the belief that a manual-labor job is the best you can do.

If you're already in your right work fit and find enjoyment in your work, getting even better at it will naturally lead you to greater levels of fulfillment. If not, no amount of time and dedication will magically create joy. We can create joy out of any occasion with a positive attitude, but believing you are destined for boring work and repeatable tasks is false.

No amount of talent and skill would have given me passion for packaging raw meat or stocking store shelves full of tuna. Maybe with the right amount of skill and reasoning, this would be true for someone else, but I highly doubt it. View certain jobs and tasks as useful stepping stones in your personal journey and nothing more.

Even if you have a passion for numbers, you probably wouldn't love doing monotonous and repetitive accounting work. Even if you love people, you might not love the mountains of paperwork involved with counseling or therapy. Even if you love animals, working at a zoo might be a nightmare for administrative reasons. Life is a mixed bag without obvious lines. There are always two sides to every story, and the right answer is discovered in the middle ground.

And if you are on the front lines right now, please hear my heart. Wherever you are right now is okay. I just want to confirm your feelings of wanting more. It's okay to want more than you have right now. In fact, I encourage it. None of us is reaching the fullest of our potential, and this includes me.

The grin-and-bear-it approach to passion isn't for the long term. Working hard and leveraging skills is admirable, and a great approach to achieving higher levels of success with whatever it is you are doing, but you may not even desire the work to begin with. I knew going into my job as an assistant community manager that I never wanted to climb the ranks and advance within. No way would I want the long working hours and increased responsibilities of a manager or regional director.

Newport's approach assumes the work you are doing now will somehow elevate you to greater heights, and that you should do whatever you can to maximize your value. But what if you prefer they ignore you so you can focus on figuring out your passions and desires? You probably don't want to be "so good they can't ignore you," as the title of his book might suggest. You may want to be just good enough to get along while you plot a better future. This isn't the ideal by any means, but it's much more likely and common.

This thought process and attitude admittedly stems from roots as a millennial and may appear selfish, but working towards your ultimate path is important, and it starts where you are right now. We don't live in the past. We live in the here and now in a transforming world. Yes, we should absolutely give our best to the work we do, but it shouldn't be everything. We should have a side hustle, a new passion, a hobby that we could eventually make our number-one thing. We should never fully depend on someone else to pay us for what we are worth because things can change on a dime.

Discovering your passion and seeking joy is more important than a raise at a job that isn't your right fit. It's more important than staying at a job long enough to be so skilled at spreadsheets that you become the king of Excel at the company. Ugh! No, thank you.

Newport says to dive in with whatever it is you are doing and develop a passion for it. I say, get busy figuring out your own passions. Develop on-the-job skills as needed to increase your "value," but don't rely on a job to tell you what you are passionate about. You don't need to suffer the opinion of a boss or coworkers to decide what you want to do with your life. It's up to you to pave your own future.

If your current work or life circumstance isn't what you want, you and only you can change that. Don't just accept the hand life dealt you; Catalyze Your Destiny! Discover what you are truly passionate about and work towards doing that one thing. And if things are okay, you need to change that too. Do you want to live for okay or for your absolute best?

I never suggest quitting, moving away from home, or making a huge life change without making a solid plan. But the truth is most people avoid taking the leap out of fear, and they opt-out of reaching their Destiny. Figuring out your Ikigai starts with loving what you do and cultivating a zest for life. The rest will follow. Life is far too short not to enjoy every minute.

The Best Option: Get Clear on What You Actually Like and Do Those Things

Let the activities you love fill your time. Discovering your passions depends on various factors, including learning and documenting what makes you the most happy. The phrase "how to be happy" is desperately searched a whopping 49,500 times per month in Google, demonstrating the enormity of the passion dilemma. It's not a simple question to answer because happiness is fleeting, inconsistent, and dependent on factors outside of our control. Just because I loved to play tennis ten years ago doesn't mean I would love teaching it today.

Life's a journey of becoming. You don't get where you're going by apparating there. You aren't Harry Potter. Hike the mountain first. Discovering personal happiness isn't something you can find with a Google search or phone call; it involves self-reflection and time to process. Even if your search leads to the best blog post ever written on finding personal happiness, you still have to take action and make a personal change.

So, how do you determine what you like? How do you determine your passions? How do you gain clarity on what brings you joy? We all have some idea of what we like, but many of us have convinced ourselves we can't have what we want, that we can't live a life on our terms. This is not true. Some passions and activities we love to do might not fit with our Ikigai, but others just might. Thinking outside the box is key, so jump on out and get your brainstorming cap on.

Start with these questions for figuring out what you love to do that might help to complete your Ikigai. Give yourself permission to dream. Channel your childlike wonder and consider what brings you unrelenting and ridiculous levels of joy:

- What makes you **laugh**? Laughter is good for the soul. Consider TV shows you love or humorous books. What moments particularly stand out that you could repeat?
- What's your favorite **activity**? Is this activity something you could help others with? This question will help you bridge the gap and connect the dots to the other points of purpose.
- What would you do if you could do **anything**? Blow the cap off your capacity by thinking of wild possibilities.
- Picture a favorite **memory** or two. What brings a smile to your face? Could you recreate this moment?
- When do you feel most **alive** and in the **flow**?

The following items bring joy to my personal life. Knowing these have helped me build a life with more of this. Knowing is the first part of the battle. Once you know what brings you the utmost joy, you can find more of it:

- Spending time with my best friend, my wife.
- Cooking and experimenting in the kitchen.
- Watching a funny show or reading a delightful book. I'm a big fan of *Harry Potter*, a multitude of science fiction and fantasy book series, and ridiculous but hilarious shows like *Impractical Jokers*.
- Spending time with friends or family. In 2020 this was often online, but it was still joyful and filled my cup.
- Giving back to others financially or with my time.
- Brainstorming in the morning over a cup of coffee and/or pondering life's deep questions at night over a drink.
- Writing and creating content to get in the flow, and losing track of time.

Dream and design the life you want to live. Discovering purpose starts with passion and knowing what brings you joy, but it doesn't end there. Learn to lead with your passions, and your purpose will grow from there. Nurture, understand, and develop your passions, and your life will become infinitely more enjoyable.

Action step: Fill in the passion part of the four points of purpose, or list what you love below. Expand your thinking outside the box. List what you enjoy doing most and revel in your unique and passionate hobbies and activities!

CHAPTER NINE: WHAT CAN I
CONTRIBUTE TO THE WORLD?

43.3% of all children born in the year 1800 died before the age of five.[14] In 1900, this number decreased to 36.20%. In 2016, this number dropped to a record low of 4.05%. Children are living past five years of age more often than ever before. But you might agree that 4% of children in the world who die before their 5th birthday is tragic and needs to change. The world is closer than ever to giving every human being their rightful shot at a long and happy life.

Solutions to major world problems are just around the corner! Mainstream media doesn't portray this hope because they make money from clickbait headlines and sensationalized news stories. As we continue to work towards this brighter future, all aspects of life will keep getting better if we want them too. You and I have a major part to play in this if we so choose.

Let me ask you a question: Would you say the world is getting better? Are stats like the child mortality rate above the norm? Probably not, right? Only 6% of US respondents to a 2016 survey thought so.[15] Turns out, those 6% were correct. The world is in fact getting better,

---

[14] "The Short History of Global Living Conditions and Why It Matters That We Know It." Our World in Data, ourworldindata.org/a-history-of-global-living-conditions-in-5-charts. Accessed 27 Dec. 2020.
[15] Roser, Max. "Share of the Population Who Think the World Is Getting Better." Our World in Data, ourworldindata.org/uploads/2016/12/Optimistic-about-the-future-2.png. Accessed 19 Feb. 2021.

in many remarkable ways. You are probably raising your eyebrow at this statement, and I don't want to lose you, so here's more data for you.

The world has improved exponentially over the last 200 years, despite the challenges we faced in 2020 with a global pandemic, Australian and Californian wildfires, the fight for racial equality, and a myriad of other issues. I took the following statistics from the same resource mentioned above, a data study conducted by Our World in Data. These facts clearly show the world is getting better. We're far from perfect as humans, but we've come a long way in the past 200 years.

- The number of people in extreme poverty 200 years ago was 89.15%. In 2015, it was 9.98%.
- Illiteracy has tanked from 87.5% to 13.98% as of 2016.
- As mentioned previously, in the year 1800, 43.3% of children died in their first five years, compared to 4% in 2016.
- The world population will not continue to grow exponentially. Women are having fewer children than ever across the globe at around 2.5 children per woman. This means the population will not continue to grow uncontrollably unless we discover ways to extend the typical human lifetime by many years.

This tool at the Gapminder website shows how greatly life expectancy has increased over the past 200 years: https://www.gapminder.org/tools

When you get the chance, click the play button and watch till the end. You'll notice a huge jump in the last 20 years. People are living longer, making more money, and having a higher quality of life than ever before. Not everything is perfect. You know this. But you aren't fighting a losing battle. The things you and I do will change the world for the better. We don't just have to believe this based on our feelings and intuition; the data shows us we can capitalize on progress and keep moving forward.

The future is bright, yes, but we still have a long way to go. The world may be getting better, but that doesn't mean we should rest. There is a lot still to do. The child mortality rate of 4% is still an absolute tragedy. It's important we know exactly what we're dealing with. There will always be things to improve, lives to change, and systems to replace. The key is picking the right battles that fit your unique identity and not getting bogged down by the weight of the world. All of your effort is not in vain.

The world needs you. It needs all your talents, skills, and abilities. It needs your expert status, your unique personality, and your vision for the future. The world needs your deep desire for positive change, your hopes, your dreams, and your enduring will to complete your goals. Hans Rosling, in his book *Factfulness*,[16] says:

> *People often call me an optimist, because I show them the enormous progress they didn't know about. That makes me angry. I'm not an optimist. That makes me sound naïve. I'm a very serious "possibilist." That's something I made up. It means someone who neither hopes without reason nor fears without reason, someone who constantly resists the overdramatic worldview. **As a possibilist, I see all this progress, and it fills me with conviction and hope that further progress is possible.** This is not optimistic. It is having a clear and reasonable idea about*

---

[16] Rosling, Hans, et al. Factfulness: Ten Reasons We're Wrong About the World—and Why Things Are Better Than You Think. Reprint, e-book, Flatiron Books, 2020.

how things are. It is having a worldview that is constructive and useful. [highlights my own].

When determining your purpose, factor in the second layer of the Ikigai, which is what the world needs. You won't find purpose by doing something that isn't needed. It's up to you to decide what is necessary. When thinking about your purpose, try to spell out what earthly needs you are filling. How will you make the world a better place?

What Does the World Need?

Raise your hand if you've ever been picked last as a member of a team? Have you been broken up with? Have you ever been fired? I get the luxury of raising my hand for all three. It stinks. Catalyzing Your Destiny doesn't work like that. YOU get to choose. It's up to you to pick one problem listed below or one of the other myriad of problems we are up against. It's up to you to make your life count by figuring out what bothers you the most and taking action to change it.

At the risk of being blunt and maybe even a little cliché , the world needs you. It will take more work than ever to close the gap and end lingering problems in this world. We can't stop moving forward despite our access to comfort and relative ease of living. I mentioned it before, but if you're reading this book, most of the problems below that still need a solution don't affect you. But it also means you might be in a prime position to solve them.

When thinking about what the world needs, start with what you know firsthand and what bothers you. Channel the fire burning within. Think about what you can't stand. If any of these problems strike a chord and light a fire in your gut, it might be a problem that needs you. Major problems still needing a solution:

- 775 million people can't read.[17]
- 1 in 3 people don't have access to safe drinking water[18]
- 2 billion people don't have access to proper sanitation[19]
- 1.3 billion still live in poverty according to the Multidimensional Poverty Index[20]
- 121 million unintended pregnancies occur each year globally, 61% of these ended in abortion.[21]
- In 2018, only 23% of the world's wilderness remains.[22]
- As of this writing, 1.7 million people have died from the COVID-19 pandemic.[23] And the numbers keep going up.

It's no question that there's an almost infinite number of ways you *could* impact the future of this Earth. But which one are you going to pick? Which one will be lucky enough to get picked by you? The list of needs could depress you or motivate you to dive in and help bring about change. I don't know about you, but over a million COVID-19 deaths hit me hard. A million people died because a few of us were careless, uninformed, and ill-prepared.

---

[17] Hammer, Kate. "Global Rate of Adult Literacy: 84 per Cent, but 775 Million People Still Can't Read." The Globe and Mail, 8 Sept. 2012, www.theglobeandmail.com/news/world/global-rate-of-adult-literacy-84-per-cent-but-775-million-people-still-cant-read/article4528932/#:%7E:text=There%20are%20775%20million%20people,to%20about%2082%20per%20cent.

[18] "1 in 3 People Globally Do Not Have Access to Safe Drinking Water – UNICEF, WHO." World Health Organization, 18 June 2019, www.who.int/news/item/18-06-2019-1-in-3-people-globally-do-not-have-access-to-safe-drinking-water-unicef-who.

[19] "Sanitation." World Health Organization, 15 June 2019, www.who.int/news-room/fact-sheets/detail/sanitation.

[20] "The 2020 Global Multidimensional Poverty Index (MPI) | Human Development Reports." UNITED NATIONS DEVELOPMENT PROGRAMME, hdr.undp.org/en/2020-MPI#fn1. Accessed 27 Dec. 2020.

[21] "Unintended Pregnancy and Abortion Worldwide." Guttmacher Institute, 17 Sept. 2020, www.guttmacher.org/fact-sheet/induced-abortion-worldwide.

[22] Fleischer, Evan. "Report: Just 23% of Earth's Wilderness Remains." Big Think, 12 Sept. 2019, bigthink.com/surprising-science/whats-left-of-the-worlds-wilderness-just-23.

[23] "Coronavirus Update (Live): 80,808,913 Cases and 1,766,743 Deaths from COVID-19 Virus Pandemic - Worldometer." Worldometer, www.worldometers.info/coronavirus. Accessed 27 Dec. 2020.

People die every day. Death is not a recent phenomenon. It's heart wrenching when someone dies before their time. Nobody should be deprived of a well-lived life full of happiness, contentment, fulfilment, and the opportunity to at least drink a healthy glass of freakin' water when they need it. Don't you agree?

If you're privileged enough to be able to read, have access to clean water, don't have to live in unclean, impoverished homes, have access to (and understand how to use) birth control, and are lucky enough to have avoided the coronavirus, you're being called to rise up. Join in. Fight. Make a difference. It's what we're here for.

The world needs... *You.*

Cogs in the Wheel

I love travelling around the world. Until I don't. It can be fun but long flights and even longer wait times are a drag. I'll never forget spending twelve hours in the Beijing airport on a layover, restlessly waiting for our next flight. I'm glad I don't solo travel. Yikes.

Invariably, the exhaustion sets in and going through security, getting questioned at customs, or the confusion of which line to get in becomes increasingly difficult. We've left bags behind on planes, spilled water on a friendly older gentleman at the start of an overnight flight, and we've gotten lost more times than we can count.

I'm lucky my partner is an amazing woman. She takes care of me, and I her. I motivate her, and she supports me. I dream, she makes sure we get it done. She plans a weekend getaway, and I put aside my writing and join her because it's always worth taking a break. We are better together. The same goes for you and me, and you and a plethora of other people.

If you're a brilliant scientist and this book serves as a call to get you to double down on your efforts to provide clean water to millions, we've both won. I've served my purpose of inspiring you, and you've served your purpose of making a direct difference. We're two cogs in the wheel, two parts of making something better out of nothing. We need each other.

There's no reason to let our weaknesses get us down or make us think we aren't doing enough or aren't good enough to make a difference. This is the power of community. It starts with personal growth but moves forward on the shoulders of partnership. Other people lift us up when we fall. We can take the baton and run with it when it's our turn.

There's no need to fill this point of purpose with every world problem. Consider what causes a fire to burn within you and make a note of those things. At the action step at the end of this chapter, get out all of your ideas. You are only one person. Yes, you are amazing, special, and full of potential, but your impact is finite. This is a hard pill to swallow, but you can't do it alone, and you don't have to. We can't solve problems in a vacuum. We need others.

You don't have to carry the weight of the world. Neither do I. Make a lasting impact, but don't think the world needs you to give your every waking hour towards its betterment. Sometimes it's more important to breathe and appreciate the beauty all around us without having to contribute. Balance is key.

If you remember this book's dedication, I shared my gratitude for two significant people in my life, Tom and Cathy. Their love, prayers, mentorship, and investment in my wife and I continue to empower us to grow, change, and influence others. Their legacy lives on inside of us and will carry on through generations. Everyone I've met that has impacted my life (good and bad) gets credit for the impact this book will have on you and the world. And yes, even those punk kids who bullied me in middle school get credit here. If you affect someone deeply, that person will impact others. The effect of your input will carry on for generations. This is powerful!

We are responsible for our words and deeds, but we don't need to feel the weight of the world. We can achieve lasting impact through steadfast nurturing and care of our purpose. The world needs you, but don't let the need overwhelm you. Move forward in the balance between living out your purpose, giving back to others, and taking a step back to let the rhythm of life carry on living through others.

Dream Big, Start Small

Dream big, change the world, put one foot forward at a time.

I often get so lost in what could be that I don't appreciate where I've been or what I'm doing. I like to think I help motivate and inspire other people to dream and shoot for the Moon. But in the end, dreaming and coming up with ideas means diddly squat if you don't do something with it. It took me a while to learn the value of starting small and moving forward on a perceived need, no matter your resources, confidence, or ability.

As my wife reminds me, "small" deeds matter. Taking the trash out helps the kitchen stay clean. Waving hello, smiling, and sincerely asking the receptionist at the doctor's office how her day is going will make her day. Leaving a positive review on Google for the local restaurant you enjoyed might mean increased business for the owner.

Dream big and start small. Don't wait for your elderly neighbor to ask you for help to mow the lawn, just do it! I've never mowed a lawn, so this advice is for me, but a small step like this could be the catalyst for the person to see the good in humanity and develop a cure for anxiety and depression. We never know how far and wide our small steps will go. We could change the world with something as simple as a smile, a raked yard, or a handwritten letter.

We won't stop here. We can't stop here. But we have to start here. Dream big and make world-altering plans, but don't get so lost in the woods you miss the trees. Start now. Put down this book. Do a small act of kindness. You'll be one step closer to your Ikigai if you do.

Action Step: How can you contribute to the world's needs? First, pause and remember what you can't stand. What makes your blood boil and your fists pumping with rage? On your Ikigai make a list of 5-10 ideas of world problems you want to solve. And then, today, do a small good deed for someone else.

CHAPTER TEN: WHAT AM I GOOD AT?

I'm terrible with directions. I get lost walking to the store, on Uber rides, and yes, I will admit to you, even inside small buildings.

One time as a freshman in college, I called my dad because my friends and I were lost. We didn't have GPS or smartphones back then. Ten years ago, Google Maps didn't exist to help me overcome the inability to navigate. My father, who was on the phone from Maine to Pennsylvania, had to get us where we needed to go.

Then, on a trip into the mountains on a snowy night in 2016, we had GPS, but it didn't matter. Where the road should have been stood an impassable fortress of snow and ice. The Blue Ridge Parkway in southern Virginia wasn't plowed, because why would it be? If we had been driving my heavy-duty, four-wheel-drive, kit-lifted Jeep Wrangler, we would have enjoyed the off-road adventure. Nope. We were stuck in our 2000 Toyota Corolla with balding tires and had to navigate a new route.

To make matters worse, at the entrance to the parkway was a sign that forever haunts me to this day:

Caution, bears in the area.

It was not a great time to have a lacking sense of direction, but I was so happy to hear "recalculating" coming from the GPS.

My confusion with directions is a family joke. Luckily, I'm so bad that I've embraced it and taken the jokes lightheartedly. I could probably get better at finding my way, and it might be a good idea to do so, but not knowing where I am is something I'm going to struggle with forever.

Knowing this gives me an advantage. I view jobs, opportunities, or new ideas through the dual lens of what I'm bad at and what I'm good at. I miss the moment and lack observational skills, but I'm great at seeing the big picture and solidifying a plan to get it done. Self-awareness sheds light on exactly the types of things you're good at and the things you struggle with. Embrace your issues by coming to grips with your limitations, and use them as a springboard for future growth.

The Anti-Strengths Assessment

You suck.

I bet you never read that in a book.

We all suck at something. Some of us suck at several things. Don't ask me to draw a picture of a cat. It will look like a blob of ink. I'm okay with this. You can be too. The more we understand what we struggle with, the more room we have for our strongest abilities to shine. If you struggle with daily life, waking up early to work a desk job, or making good eating decisions, odds are you are unaware of your abilities that will help you overcome these deficits. Maybe you're a night owl entrepreneur who needs to surround yourself with healthy food. You owe it to yourself and the world to get to know what you suck at so you can be the best possible version of you with what you're good at.

There are no anti-strengths or anti-skills assessments on the World Wide Web. They wouldn't be any fun to take, because who wants to know their weaknesses or dwell on what they aren't good at? To be fair, I don't want to spend too much time on it either. The idea isn't to be negative, but you have to get the bad out of the way first to make room for the good. Learn and know your weaknesses and then move forward on the path to growth.

So, real quick, think about your worst quality traits and what you wish you could improve in yourself. The next step is to embrace the suck and be okay with your inadequacies. You are the sum of the whole, and this includes the bad. Optimism beats pessimism any day, but it's tastier with a bit of reality sprinkled in.

I'll share my weaknesses below so you don't feel alone. I'm terrible at:

- Directions
- Swimming
- Acting normal at a party
- Remembering to smile while I'm thinking hard
- Consistency
- Responding to people right away when they contact me
- Enjoying the moment
- Correcting people even when it's in their best interest

It's easy to get bogged down with what you're bad at, but this doesn't justify not doing anything. The whole point of looking at your skills and getting to know yourself better is to weed through opportunities and pick the ideas you're best suited to. If your next steps are going to crash against your weaknesses, be prepared and get help, or come up with a new game plan. Don't beat your head against the wall unless you know you're close to a breakthrough.

What Am I Good At?

Phew!! That's over. Now let's get to the good stuff. Now that you know what *not* to put on the third part of your Ikigai, let's dig in and come up with a list of skills, strengths, and positive attributes you can add to your personal Ikigai. Follow this simple process to brainstorm ideas of exactly what you're good at:

1. Start with a five-minute brain dump. Write down everything you can think of that you're good at. Don't limit your thinking by comparing answers to the other Ikigai points, we'll do that later.
2. Use any of the self-discovery tools listed previously. Both the MBTI and CliftonStrengths are great starting points for what you are naturally good at. Dig in and get to know more about your type and strengths and what makes you uniquely awesome.
3. Ask a friend or two what they think you're good at. Similar to the icebreaker question in the first section, this will give you a mix of surprising and affirmative answers.
4. Dig deeper: Think of three to four of your major life points (wedding, college, high school, etc.). What were you good at then? What did you most enjoy about those times?
5. Need even more prompts? Think about what you're good at in school, at home, at work, when hanging out with friends, when you're happy, or when you're sad. Think about what you're doing when you're in the flow and time passes by like a lightning bolt. Imagine the moments of sheer joy and consider why you experienced that emotion.

It's a lot more fun thinking of what you're good at, huh? I definitely want you to spend more time here than on what you're bad at. It's important to focus on strengths to complete your Ikigai. Strengths complete you and give you energy. Knowing weaknesses is important, but you'll thrive from the point of strength.

I'll share a few of my strengths below as an example. I'm good at:

- Throwing a frisbee
- Taking action and getting things done
- Feeling empathy
- Dreaming about the future
- Communicating, especially with tough conversations
- Halo
- Tennis
- Walking
- Eating healthy
- Sleeping in
- Handling emergencies
- Hustling
- Remembering people's names

When you do this exercise yourself, think of as many items as possible. Fill out this Ikigai section with abandon. You are good at a lot of things. Write them down and enjoy that smile that's on your face right now. It's okay to think about what you're good at. You deserve to bask in your awesomeness for a few seconds. And contrary to what I said earlier, you don't suck, not at all. You are so much more amazing than you know.

This step is just one part of putting your purpose puzzle together, but you are getting closer. We're almost ready to analyze how to intersect the four points, but you're doing great. These baby steps might seem tedious (although I hope they're fun) but they matter. Why? Because you matter!

It matters that you are good at throwing a baseball because your son wants to play catch with you. It matters that you love to encourage others because your significant other needs kind words to keep moving toward their goals. It matters that you stopped to help the lady whose car broke down because she was one bad situation away from ending it all.

You are hope. You are someone's best chance at a new tomorrow. You are powerful and unstoppable. Your skills and strengths contribute not only to making the world better, but to helping individuals one person at a time. Never forget the impact your positive skills will have on the world.

Action Step: Using what you learned about yourself from the first section, write down on your Ikigai or in bullets below what you're good at. Don't limit your answers by level of greatness, good is good enough.

CHAPTER ELEVEN: WHAT CAN I GET PAID TO DO?

I vividly remember the first time I made money online. I was dancing with my wife at my cousin's wedding in March 2015. Spinning and twirling, whooping and hollering, we were having a grand old time. On a break, a glance at the Google AdSense app on my phone stunned me. I had earned thirteen cents from an ad click! Someone found their way to my website, clicked on an ad, and sent thirteen shiny new pennies my way.

I jumped back on the dance floor and danced the night away with jubilee. It meant nothing, but it meant everything. I had tangible proof it was possible to make money online. thirteen cents isn't even enough to buy one of those little green sticks to keep your Starbucks coffee warm, but it was the spark I needed to keep moving forward toward my dream.

My dream of working online has taken many iterations since that fateful ad click. I've tried many avenues, most of which have failed. I've also had a bunch of success points and major breakthroughs. Through it all, I've learned one simple truth: Anyone can get paid for doing work; you just have to know your stuff, work relentlessly, and not let setbacks set you back.

I've worn so many hats throughout the last several years, almost none of which I deserved to wear initially, but it doesn't matter. "Fake it 'til you make it" might sound like a millennial excuse for not being prepared, but it forms the base for the approach I want you to take.

Don't worry so much about whether you can do the job. Believe that if someone else can do it, you certainly can too. A strong work ethic and a killer drive for success will take you far.

In her popular book *Everything is Figureoutable*,[24] Marie Forleo, shares:

You can do whatever you set your mind to if you just roll up your sleeves, get in there, and do it. Everything is figureoutable.

Self-awareness, confidence, and relentless desire will bring you all the money you'll ever need. I realize this may sound too good to be true, but it's not. If you start with what you're good at and develop deeper understanding and aptitude, the world will open before you. You will figure it out. It will take a mix of skills and abilities, but more than anything, it will take confidence in knowing who you are and what you can provide.

What Do You Want to Get Paid For?

You can choose what to give back to the world. You don't need to wait on other people to point you toward your Destiny. You are in the driver's seat of your life and your finances. You get to choose what to get paid for. This is true for you right now, even if you don't know it.

Now is one of the best times in human history to take action to find better work. Discover work you love that fits your overall purpose. Work no longer needs to be just a 9-5 that pays the bills. It can and should be so much more. And it's not only possible, it's accessible to you right now. With the internet and the expanded knowledge and

---

[24] Forleo, Marie. Everything Is Figureoutable. e-book, Portfolio, 2020.

distribution of remote work, people are finding better work/life balance than ever before. According to a recent survey of 4,000+ remote workers, 73% said that working from home improved their work-life balance.[25] When you can work from anywhere, the world quickly becomes open to you. Taylor Pearson, in his book *End of Jobs*,[26] adds:

"What has changed is that the kind of work needed to advance society taps into fundamental human drives now. Complex, entrepreneurial work is both more valuable and more in line with traditional human drives."

How many people do you know who use their college degrees? Have you or someone you know pursued a master's degree or their doctorate and then wondered what to do next? It doesn't mean as much as it used to. It's great to have a degree and even just having a BA can give you a leg up in the interview process, but this advantage wasn't worth four years of my life and the crushing debt of student loans. Before you further your education, make sure you're aware of other options and the changing tides. Don't follow the crowd and miss the declining value and rising risk of higher education. It's something no one wants to talk about, and college may absolutely be the best decision for you, but be clear on your why.

The undeniable way forward is becoming an expert in yourself and your unique contribution to the world. It's on you to figure out how to reorganize your daily life to live out your purpose. Call it entrepreneurial or call it whatever you want, complex work not easily replaceable or replicable by machines is the way of the future. The

[25] Pelta, Rachel. "FlexJobs Survey: Productivity, Work-Life Balance Improves During Pandemic." FlexJobs Job Search Tips and Blog, 28 Dec. 2020, www.flexjobs.com/blog/post/survey-productivity-balance-improve-during-pandemic-remote-work.
[26] Pearson, Taylor. The End of Jobs: Money, Meaning and Freedom Without the 9-to-5. e-book, Three Magnolia LLC, 2015.

barriers to entry are lower than ever. We have an open sea of possibilities in front of us to give back to the world, share our knowledge in person and online, and create great things. All you need is a laptop, a connection to the internet, and the drive and determination to discover your place.

You can manifest your ideal "job" or line of work. Paying work will come purely from whatever it is you want to do. This truth and mindset might be foreign to you, but it's one I implore you to take to heart, or at least consider. You get to choose what to get paid for. It's not based on any one skill, degree, or outside influence. It's solely based on your choice.

This process doesn't involve magic. No opportunity will pop into existence overnight (at least at first). It always takes more grit and determination than you're able to give, but opportunities will open up before you when you least expect it. You likely cannot do what you want right now, but with time, anything is possible. The problem is you're going to be in the same place in six months as you are right now unless you get clear on what YOU want to get paid for and then start working toward that reality.

Remember the work history test you did earlier? It will help you here, and it's almost like cheating. The best way to get started in thinking about work you can get paid for is to look at what former employers or clients have paid you for. What work did you enjoy doing that also helped pay the bills? What strengths, skills, and abilities helped you to get paid for these tasks? What could you get paid to do right now?

You can get paid for anything you do that's a service for others. If you know how to do it, enjoy it, and people need it (Ikigai one to three), they will pay for it. This is the incredible flexibility of the fourth point of purpose. With the dawn of the sharing economy, the end of normal jobs as we know it, and the inevitability of remote work, the future looks bright for anyone with the desire to give back and serve others. The easier the work, the less you'll get paid (business 101), but those first few pennies can be a game-changer. It's a reality that's possible for anyone with the gumption to go after it.

Don't stop short of your dreams because you're worried about money. Move past this fear. This isn't a book about how to earn money online. It's a subject I'm fascinated by and fairly familiar with, but it's not the big picture. The crucial point, and the one I want you to leave this chapter with, is that letting money issues stop you from chasing your dreams is not only a terrible excuse but also a lie.

You Don't Have to Be the Best

This fourth Ikigai point is where many people get needlessly stuck. Just because you can't get paid for something now doesn't mean you can't work towards that possibility for the future. I could eventually teach others how to write books if I wanted to. I could teach people how to play Catan competitively, how to become a digital nomad, or how to find the motivation to run a half marathon during a global pandemic.

I'm not the world's best author. I still get beat when I play Catan. I'm not an expert on how to become a digital nomad (I just did it). And I'm far from the fastest and most consistent runner. But I could still coach new authors (which I've done), build an introductory course for Catan, or create a quick-start runner's guide for tall guys. I could make money with any of these examples if I chose to dig deep, focus on that one passion area, and provide value.

We can turn our passions and knowledge into paying gigs as long as the quest matches our desires, regardless of our skill level. We need not rely on the government or a college degree for our careers provided we have something unique to offer the world and we discover what that something is. Luckily, once you learn how to infuse your personality and strengths into your work, you'll gain insight into your personal superpowers and never look back.

You may never be the best at anything. Being number one doesn't matter and shouldn't stop you. You don't have to be the best; you just have to be you. Your combination of skills is unique and, let me say it, pretty outstanding. The tennis great Roger Federer can't do some things I can. He'd wallop me in tennis, but I'd crush him in Settlers of Catan or *Star Wars* trivia. He's a normal guy who focused hard on one thing and became extremely talented.

Federer maximized his four points of purpose because he obviously loves what he does. The smile on his face while he's playing is evidence of his personal enjoyment. Millions of others benefit from the competitive entertainment value when he crushes other skilled opponents. He gets paid handsomely for a job well done. He's not only good at tennis, but one of the best in the world.

Merge what you're good at and can get paid to do with your identity. You can get paid for whatever work you choose, so long as you put in time and relentless effort. But here's the key: It's not just the combination of time and effort needed to get good at one particular skill; it's the time and effort to build a set of abilities cohesive with your personality and innate strengths. You are the infusion of everything you were, are, and want to be.

What I've Been Paid For

What follows is a non-exhaustive list of what I've gotten paid for in the past five years. I'm nothing special, and that's the point. Adopting an abundance mindset starts with becoming a possibilist. You, too, can have a piece of the pie. You don't need to be the best at anything, you just need to find your best work fit.

Use this list to remind you of your own skills ("I've done that!"), to give you some fun ideas for making money ("That looks like fun!"), or to show what's possible when you Catalyze Your Destiny ("I'm so ready!").

- Audio engineering
- Audiobook editing
- Google advertising
- Affiliates
- Various bookselling (non-fiction, journals, notebooks, etc.)
- Online courses
- Copywriting
- Ghostwriting
- Content creation
- Digital marketing work
- Social media managing
- Consultations/coaching

Does this list get your mouth watering for what's possible? You might be familiar with several of these items, or you think you could do them too. Money is a barrier to overcome, not an impediment to progress. Find the thing you do well that also brings in the dollars. Do enough of this thing to feed your bigger dreams. Eventually, you'll only have to do the work you love because it pays you.

Action Step: On your Ikigai or in bullets, jot down some ideas about what others will pay you to do. Let your notes reflect your work history and what you'd like to get paid for in the future.

_____

_____

_____

CHAPTER TWELVE: COMPLETING YOUR IKIGAI

Don't you sometimes wish you could skip growing pains and challenges? Me too.

"My soup isn't warm enough," our resident Jane said to me one evening during dinner. I could see the rolling steam coming off the mug of hot soup, but of course I said, "I'm sorry about that, I'll be right back with a fresh cup." You knew stress was at an all-time high when you almost couldn't resist rolling your eyes at a sweet old lady.

"Who wanted the sliced tomato!?" our forgetful manager heartily called out to a full dining room from the kitchen door. No one responded, but those who heard him laughed nervously. In the stressful environment, how could one remember who had asked for tomato slices? The resident who asked for it, God bless him or her, had probably forgotten themselves!

"Denise, would you mind giving these friendly people a look around?" I asked my sister one busy Saturday afternoon. Denise did not work at the community, but she quickly learned that if you came for a visit, we might just put you to work! Things were so hectic my gracious sister, instead of enjoying her visit, had to give a tour to a nice young couple even though it was her first time in the building.

Sometimes the most disconnected jobs, hobbies, or life events coalesce to get us where we need to go. Your next step doesn't have to be your last. It might just be a painful steppingstone on the road to finding out what it is you were meant to do. Take heart in everything you do and have done. Nothing is without merit or without value. Every job, every hobby, every life activity is fueling the soul fire of your purpose.

I never would have guessed my time as a marketing manager at the retirement community would have paved the way for my future of being an entrepreneur. Sure, I would grow, but I never thought it would be a pivotal point in my journey. Looking back, I'm glad I didn't skip it, despite the overwhelming struggle.

When I left the normal workforce and launched into entrepreneurship in 2017, I quickly learned it wouldn't be smooth sailing. Far from it. It would be easier in many ways than any of my past jobs, but the change brought with it a myriad of unexpected challenges. To my shock, the skills I needed most in this new line of "work" were the same skills I had been learning all along. Discipline, trust building, hustle, understanding, and problem solving were just a few of the skills I would have to cultivate and master to find success.

I believe God has a habit of putting us exactly where we need to be when we need to be there. You might call it karma or the universe aligning for you, but I'm willing to bet you agree it's the things we struggle through that have the strongest impact on who we become. Nobody wants to deal with challenges or painful situations, but the iron is stronger after the fire.

Determining your unique life purpose is a lifelong endeavor that requires multiple steps of action, failure, and repetition to get right. Get it right, and you'll live longer too.[27] But I'll warn you right off

---

[27] Gander, Kashmira. "People With a Sense of Purpose Live Longer, Study Suggests." Newsweek, 24 May 2019, www.newsweek.com/people-sense-purpose-live-longer-study-suggests-1433771.

the bat, you might spend your life seeking purpose and never be 100% clear about what you should do with your life. Your Ikigai will fade in and out, change, and might even look completely different in five years. Your future is unlimited, and so are the potential variations of your Ikigai, the good and bad, challenging and fulfilling, painful and enjoyable, fascinating and frightening.

The best action to take is to continue to learn and grow. In the next chapter, we'll take a step back and share several examples of what a completed Ikigai looks like for real people, so you can envision what shape yours will take. In this chapter, I want to give you concrete action steps to merge the four points of purpose by cross-examination.

A few notes before we continue:

- It's hard to find a career or job that fits all four points of the Ikigai. You're much more likely to unlock purpose by forging your own way, OR by working for/with a strong leader who wants you to become your best self. Unfortunately, most companies and leaders won't fit this bill, and you'll be just another number. This is not always the case, but as long as you are working for someone else you'll be under their umbrella of values, decisions, and direction.
- Discovering your Ikigai is an iterative process. It will change. It won't come together one day and then be the same for years. You'll constantly be growing into your Ikigai.
- Don't seek perfection, even if you're a 1 on the Enneagram. Don't worry about making the perfect plan, or waiting for the time to be right. Taking action is the best catalyst for growth and understanding. Sometimes you have to embrace the suck and get your hands dirty to figure out what you are supposed to be doing.

139

Ikigai Crossovers, The Final 6 Questions to Fill in the Ikigai

Now the rubber meets the road and it gets even more fun. You're going to compare each of the four points to discover crossover ideas. Get into future mode here by envisioning what you want your ideal Ikigai to be. Don't limit yourself to what's immediately possible! Instead, get outside of the box and generate great ideas. This will take practice, but take the time to do the work and you'll gain insights and new direction.

Now that you have the outer edges of the Ikigai filled out, it's time to crossover each point with the other. This will take some time, so have patience with it. There's nothing I hate more than an online test, quiz, or worksheet that says, "Easy to finish in 15 minutes!" when I'm struggling to even start within 15 minutes, let alone finish the darn thing. Discovering your purpose is a lofty goal that no single test, book, course, or person will unveil. You must determine it yourself via introspection and experience.

Fill out the points by answering with bullets. Use the diagram if you get stuck, but if the visual aid confuses or doesn't help, stick to writing notes or talking over it with a friend over a meal. What you're looking for are connection points that are music to your ears. You want the ideas that make you say "Well, that's something I could do!" Look for patterns with your answers between the points and see the big picture. With these comparisons, you'll quickly see what will work and what won't.

Quickly work your way through these questions to scoop up any previously missed ideas. Grab the list you created from the previous chapters or recall those sweet memories. Consider how each individual idea will carry over to complete your Ikigai:

1. What worldly needs can your passion meet?
2. What will someone pay you for that involves your passion?
3. What do you love to do and are good at?
4. What does the world need that you can get paid for?
5. Do you have a skill or talent that fits a bigger world need?
6. What are some of your highest-paid abilities?

If you can answer even some of the above questions, you'll see your Ikigai taking shape. Hopefully, you're getting excited about the possibilities before you. Now take time to consider and answer these probing questions before moving on.

Whatever You Do, Get Started

Now, the ultimate question: Do any of your ideas match all four Ikigai points? How about three points? Have you found your Ikigai, or are you close? Congrats! Your hard work is paying off. After analyzing the first set of crossovers, have a short list of ideas or activities that might be your Ikigai. If you have a huge list, continue to cross-check and eliminate items from contention, but even getting to three out of four is a great starting point.

With three out of four, you are giving yourself a solid chance at success and incredible life fulfillment. You will learn to love something if it meets every other need. You will get paid. You'll fill a worldly need. And you will train up to get good at something. Often, you have to get started to fill that last void.

If you end up with less than three out of four, you're already sinking and will struggle to reach your Ikigai. Go back to the drawing board, come up with a few new ideas, and try to get to three of four matches. And remember, you don't have to be merging any of the four points right now, but think about what you want your future to look like.

Of course, you can't stay at only three out of four forever. Without loving what you do, you'll feel empty. Without meeting a world need, it will feel pointless. Without adequate skill, you'll feel useless. Without money, you'll crash and burn and financial security will evade you. Eventually, you'll find your Ikigai when all four points live in harmony and connectedness. It's a lofty goal, and not everyone will attain it, but it's worth the pursuit.

Focused pursuit doesn't mean I can't still have passions here and there. Indeed, I enjoy coaching other people in writing a book when they ask, but I'd much rather be leading people to talk about their deeper purpose and big life goals. This is where my purpose lies, in the heart of helping people to find their why. Just because you can pursue something doesn't mean you should. It's up to you to determine your values and decide if a particular Destiny is worth going after.

For those who need to hear it most, this advice will come as no surprise. Just. Do. Something. Start and figure it out as you go. As you build upon talents, enhance your skills, and craft new abilities, doors will open for you.

Don't let perfection be the enemy of done. No matter what you decide to do, get it done. Don't waste time trying to make sure it's perfect. It won't be perfect. No matter how much time and energy you put into something, it won't be perfect. If you look hard enough, I guarantee you'll find some sort of error or typo within this book. I don't like it, but I've accepted it. Do your due diligence and absolutely put your best foot forward, but don't let the quest for perfection derail your action train.

The Final Problem

What if my idea hits all four points, and I still don't want to do it? Great question!

I love tennis. I'm good at it. People could benefit from it. And I could get paid to do it either via coaching, creating how-to videos, or another idea. I could list a few other things that tick the Ikigai box on paper, but I know I don't want to do them. Listen to this intuition! Listen to what you already know to be true. Just because it hits all four boxes or matches every suggestion I've given here, trust your gut first. Leave preconceived notions and biases at the door, but always move forward with what you know to be true about yourself.

This final problem is challenging because we might not have a lot to pick from without a smattering of life experiences. This is one reason the age-old advice of "try new things" isn't a cliche but ridiculously important to remember. The more you know about yourself and what you like and don't like, the easier it will be to cast aside weaker Ikigais for the right one.

Solving the final problem and choosing one lifelong purpose will come from trial and error. You'll likely have multiple false starts, failures, and other problems along the way. You'll think you're on target, and then a major roadblock will cause you to question everything. It's at this point you need to strive forward and keep up the momentum. This is where you'll channel your action-taking prowess and forge ahead. With action and perseverance, any goal is within your grasp.

Action Step: Before you move on, what is one nugget you'll take away from learning about the Ikigai?

_____

_____

_____

CHAPTER THIRTEEN: IS IT POSSIBLE TO LIVE OUT MY IKIGAI?

There are days I wish I could channel the genius of Tony Stark, work out with the strength of the Hulk, or have hair as golden as Chris Hemsworth's, *cough*, I mean Thor's. I fell in love with Marvel movies when Robert Downey Jr. appeared as Iron Man in 2008 while I was still in college. The movies are epic, the plots are on point, but the true value comes from each of the characters in the universe and the actors and actresses who play them.

It's beautiful to see the end results when a big project comes together. The brilliant writers, creative set designers, vision-driven directors, and magnanimous casts are just a few of the pieces to Marvel's unprecedented success in the film industry. While the superheroes displayed on screen don't actually exist, the magic behind their creation involves a larger community full of people who are living out their Ikigai. When you discover your Ikigai and live it out, you're contributing to something greater than yourself.

In this chapter we'll delve into the lives of five real-life superheroes, people who never should have had a chance at greatness, but shouted "NO!" and pushed forward anyway and found their Ikigai after overcoming major trials and hardship.

These are the real heroes we will learn from today. We will learn how they kept moving forward despite everything and everyone telling them otherwise. We'll learn how they channeled their pain into life-giving energy to overcome adversity despite unfair life circumstances.

These stories are not equal, but such is the point. Being born without arms or legs is a serious difficulty that I wouldn't wish on my arch-nemesis. Homelessness, shark attacks, and a forced stay at a concentration camp were some of the challenges faced by our heroes. We ALL have unique life circumstances holding us back. The key is to accept our circumstances for what they are, use them if we can, and push forward no matter what.

As we close section two with these everyday heroes, I hope these stories help funnel energy into your life purpose. If I can do it, so can you. If they can do it, maybe anyone can. We'll learn from Nick Vujicic, a man born without arms or legs, but who still became a husband, father, international speaker, and author. We'll dive into the life of Liz Murray and how she went from homelessness to Harvard. We'll learn the power of setting massive life goals from Jessica Cox. We'll uncover the secret drive that kept Bethany Hamilton on the waves, despite every reason to stay on dry land. We'll learn from Victor E. Frankl how you can overcome anything in life with the power of a deeper purpose.

Let's dive in and learn from these five authentic heroes.

1) Nick Vujicic

It's a lie to think you're not good enough. It's a lie to think you're not worth anything. If you can't get a miracle, become one.

—*Nick Vujicic, Life Without Limits*

Nick was born without arms or legs. Nick and his family were told he wouldn't lead a "normal" life. The doctors couldn't have been more correct. Nick's life has been as far from normal as you can get, and now we all benefit. He has lived a life of impact and miracles. His "normal" life has gone far beyond anyone's wildest expectations.

I had the pleasure of meeting Nick in person. I got to give him a hug. It was amazing. It's an experience I won't ever forget. He radiated joy, love, and compassion. You could tell he was tired from speaking for hours, but it didn't matter. Everyone in the room treasured his gifts. It's just a guess, but I bet it's these hugs that keep him moving forward. Knowing that he gets to change lives and meet those he helps has to be huge.

In his book *Life Without Limits*,[28] which I loved and highly recommend, Nick shares his overriding desire to walk on his own two legs one day. He prays for it constantly. He works towards it by trying new technologies. But even though he has yet to find a solution, he's found incredible motivation and drive from telling his story and by leaning into his ability to speak and influence.

This little guy walking around on top of a table captivated me. He discovered his purpose of public speaking and leaned into it with all his heart. He loves it because he gets to share his story. It meets a world need because he fills people with hope and inspiration. He gets paid well to do the work with engagements all over the world. He's skilled at it because when he speaks, you listen.

Nick has written several books, speaks around the world, and has a wife and family of his own. What more might he accomplish? If he can do it, why not you?

---

[28] Vujicic, Nick. Life Without Limits: Inspiration for a Ridiculously Good Life. Reprint, WaterBrook, 2012.

2) Liz Murray

> *Instead, what I was beginning to understand was that however things unfolded from here on, whatever the next chapter was, my life could never be the sum of one circumstance. It would be determined, as it had always been, by my willingness to put one foot in front of the other, moving forward, come what may.*

> —*Liz Murray, Breaking Night: A Memoir of Forgiveness, Survival, and My Journey from Homeless to Harvard*

Raised by drug-addicted parents, Liz became homeless at fifteen. Her mother had just died of HIV, and she and her father moved into a homeless shelter. Liz attended a local high school and quickly graduated. She dug deep and kept going, despite everything going against her, and got a scholarship to Harvard.

From an interview with BBC,[29] we learn that what motivated Liz was talking about her past events and what she overcame to take the next step with her life. It's fascinating that the very thing helping her to conquer was... talking about what she had to conquer. Liz turned an untenable situation on its head and created her own momentum. She channeled difficult life circumstances into a winning scenario. She refused to give up no matter how low she got.

Liz graduated from Harvard in 2009 and founded her company, Manifest Living. She is now living out her purpose as an inspirational speaker, bestselling author, mother, and winner of Oprah's Chutzpah Award.

---

[29] Lee, Dave. "How Liz Murray Went from Homelessness to Harvard." BBC News, 8 Feb. 2011, www.bbc.com/news/world-us-canada-12367021.

3) Jessica Cox

*It's only human to have low moments in life because if you don't,
then you won't feel the high, exciting times.*

—*Jessica Cox*

Jessica Cox was born without arms because of a rare birth defect. Just
like Nick, she had to overcome physical limitations right from birth.
She never had the chance to experience life with arms. I can't help
but feel pity for those who suffer right from birth. It gives me
enormous respect and admiration when they're able to overcome and
embrace their purpose.

Jessica set a huge goal, one she had no business reaching for. She
would get her pilot's license; her feet would do the work! She reached
for greater heights and higher goals than made sense for someone
with her limitations. Isn't this a ridiculous or overzealous goal for
someone without arms?

Yes.

But she did it anyway!

It took her three years (the average time is six months) and multiple
complications and setbacks because of her condition, but she did it.
She completed her major life goal by getting her pilot's license. Oh,
she also holds a black belt, is a motivational speaker, and has her
SCUBA certification. Don't mess with Jessica!

4) Bethany Hamilton

> *Life is a lot like surfing… When you get caught in the impact zone, you've got to just get back up. Because you never know what may be over the next wave.*
>
> —*Bethany Hamilton, Soul Surfer: A True Story of Faith, Family, and Fighting to Get Back on the Board*[30]

Bethany had her arm bitten off by a shark at thirteen years old in 2003. It's bad enough being born without an appendage, but can you imagine the horror of an accident that leaves you without one of your arms? I can't. Bethany moved beyond this event and turned it into something positive. She not only overcame, she went to even greater heights. She used her difficulties to fuel her search for purpose.

It was her foundation of faith and uncanny perseverance that kept her going. Bethany was up surfing again only one month after the shark attacked her. I'm not a fan of the water at all. If a shark attacked me, I'd give up surfing forever. No way would I go back out there. But just thirty days later, she was fearlessly back up and surfing again.

We might never have known Bethany Hamilton if she didn't go through this event and then overcome it. If she had never gone back out on the waves, she would have been nothing but a tragic accident in the history books. The story she would have told is why she didn't surf anymore and why she was afraid of the water. It's a story to which we can relate, and no one would blame her for following this narrative.

But no! Bethany overcame her roadblock to impact the rest of us. Her perseverance and fearless living are legendary character traits,

---

[30] Hamilton, Bethany, et al. Soul Surfer: A True Story of Faith, Family, and Fighting to Get Back on the Board. Illustrated, MTV Books, 2006.

and she gets to live a life of surfing, writing, speaking, and inspiring others. She has achieved worldwide fame for her positive attitude, wrote a book about her traumatic experience, competed on the popular show *The Amazing Race*, and has competed professionally in surfing.

5) Viktor E. Frankl

> *Everything can be taken from a man but one thing: the last of the human freedoms—to choose one's attitude in any given set of circumstances; to choose one's own way.*

> *Those who have a 'why' to live can bear with almost any 'how.'*

> *—Viktor E. Frankl, Man's Search for Meaning*

Between 1942 and 1945, Viktor E. Frankl was imprisoned at Nazi-controlled concentration camps, including Auschwitz. The Nazis killed his wife and entire family. After his three-year horrifying stint at the camp, he wrote the popular book *Man's Search for Meaning* in nine days, using the notes he had taken mostly in his head.

He credits his ability to keep moving forward despite all odds to his desire to tell his story and share the psychological discoveries he made. Meditating on his love for his beloved, having the courage to face life's challenges, and understanding his "why" helped get him through.

He made his "why" the need to survive to tell his tale, which helped him keep moving forward despite all the odds. He believed he had a purpose yet to fulfil, and this carried him through unspeakable pain and difficulties. His idea of holding onto a future goal and working towards it relentlessly helped him survive against the odds. He turned something terrible into a book which has helped millions find purpose and understanding.

You: Hero and Ikigai Master

I hope these heroes have helped establish the power of the human will for life, the resilience we all have access to, and the benefit of moving forward despite the odds. But the story isn't over. It's your turn to become the hero in the story. Now, with the ultimate power of self-discovery mixed with the secret of the Ikigai, you're unstoppable. Nothing can stand in the way of reaching your dreams as long as you keep moving forward.

You may not have had the hard life of some of these heroes, but you've had hardships and setbacks. We all have. No one is immune to the trials and tribulations of life. What's hard for me might be easy for you, and vice versa. No one's challenges are the same. If what you're going through right now is the hardest thing you've ever faced, you're allowed to struggle. I've never had my arm bitten off by a shark, and I've never been homeless. That doesn't mean my struggles are any less meaningful or challenging to me. It's okay to struggle with the cards life is dealing you. We all face different roadblocks on life's journey.

What is the obstacle you need to overcome? Don't make the mistake of negatively comparing yourself to the heroes listed here. Instead, channel their perseverance, positivity, and tenacity to keep going no matter what. You will have setbacks. Things will suck. But embrace the suck and tackle your challenges head on.

It's what we do with the challenges that matters. It's the next step that matters. It's taking what you've learned, not only from this book but from your trials and experience, and making a plan to move forward. Most books end here before things get good. Most people will stop reading as soon as the movie of their life requires hard work and input. Most people stop living once they reach a comfort level.

But not you. Right? You want to Catalyze your Destiny! It's time to go. It's time to begin. It's time to leave normal behind and get dangerous... Let's make a plan, shall we?

Action Step: Who are your heroes? Write a few sentences about one person who has profoundly impacted your life.

PART THREE:

LAUNCH INTO ACTION AND IGNITE YOUR SOUL FIRE

CHAPTER FOURTEEN: THE UNSTOPPABLE
POWER OF DESIRE

If you want something bad enough, nothing will stop you. Take to heart these words from Walt Disney: *"All our dreams can come true if we have the courage to pursue them."* If we have the courage to pursue our dreams, nothing will get in our way. The seven-time Super Bowl winning, greatest of all time, NFL quarterback Tom Brady, shows us how this aim is possible for anyone.

199th draft pick. An okay arm. The second slowest quarterback at the 2000 NFL combine. A hard pass if there ever was one. Yet University of Michigan's quarterback Tom Brady became one of the greatest quarterbacks of all time in the NFL. And he's still winning today, having just won yet another Super Bowl at forty-three, older than any Super Bowl winning player ever by two years.

It's not just because Bill Belichick (arguably the best coach in sports) gave him a chance. It's not just because the stars aligned and he proved himself. It's not just because he had great teammates. Brady seized his chance to be great and merged it with an insatiable desire to be the best. He may have had luck and timing on his side, but he was ready to capitalize on the moment when his mentor, Drew Bledsoe, was injured in the second game of the 2001 season. Brady took his spot and never looked back.

We all have our story, and I started at a place where I always felt like I was looking up at everybody. I was looking up at everybody in high school and then college and certainly when I started in the pros. Through a lot of help and a lot of support, I just learned, and I kept trying to get a little bit better and a little bit better and keep growing and keep evolving. I still feel like I'm trying to do that today.[31] *— Tom Brady*

It's hard to get much better than seven wins in ten Super Bowl appearances, but Brady is always pushing for more. Old habits die hard. Brady proves you don't have to be the best, the brightest, and the greatest from the start. He shows that wherever you are, you can channel your desire for more into real-life progress. We should take this advice to heart and breathe deep. Wherever we're at now is okay, but we need not stay there.

I'm a huge fan of this former New England Patriots quarterback (and a bit ticked he went to Tampa Bay for the 2020 season). Even though he had the least promising career of any NFL player before his time, he used the power of a focused desire to achieve incredible heights. What set him apart was an uncanny belief in what was possible. He worked hard and set his sights on his goal and never gave up.

Brady is a possibilist who doesn't believe you can't have something. Brady teaches through his actions, positive habits, and a winning mindset. He doesn't indulge in pizza and beer during the offseason. He refuses to believe he's reached the zenith of his capability. The power of his desire, his clear purpose, and his uncanny work ethic paved the way to an incredible future. The same is possible for you.

To craft a plan for living out your purpose (or discovering what that purpose is), you have to want it. Without a clear and insatiable desire,

---

[31] London, Adam. "How Tom Brady Feels About His Famous NFL Scouting Combine Photo." NESN.Com, 28 Dec. 2019, nesn.com/2019/12/how-tom-brady-feels-about-his-famous-nfl-scouting-combine-photo.

your goal won't come to fruition. Your desire can't be weak; you have to want it with every fiber of your being. Your desire for growth and change will be the why that fuels your how.

Desire vs. Wishful Thinking

In his book *Think and Grow Rich*,[32] author and businessman Napoleon Hill said:

"The starting point of all achievement is desire. Keep this constantly in mind. Weak desires bring weak results, just as a small fire makes a small amount of heat."

Wishing and hoping for something to happen is the opposite of channeling desire. I could wish for money and dream about a stork who drops off a basketful of hundred-dollar bills, but Larry the Stork doesn't exist. He won't be dropping off a package in this reality. This is a ridiculous example, and no one believes in money-carrying storks, but sometimes we live our lives as if it's true. I know that I have.

You can wish for something to happen, but if you don't have the deeper desire that creates opportunity, it often won't work out. Instead, if you learn how to channel desire, you will manifest your Destiny. I know that sounds a little woo-woo and out there, but it isn't. It goes beyond hope and wishing for something to happen; it's manifesting it for yourself by building the future by noticing and taking advantage of possibilities.

Wishing is passive. Hoping is soul-enriching, but doesn't get a lot

---

[32] Hill, Napoleon, and Arthur Pell. Think and Grow Rich: The Landmark Bestseller Now Revised and Updated for the 21st Century (Think and Grow Rich Series). Revised and Enlarged, e-book, TarcherPerigee, 2005.

done if an action doesn't take place. Passive living won't get you from here to there and back again. Consider adopting or changing the following action-oriented mantra to fit your purposes:

I want this goal more than anything. I will think about it while eating. I will fill my journal with ideas. I will dream about accomplishing my goal. I will work my butt off and do whatever it takes to get to the finish line.

Desire is rooted in action. There's no such thing as an overnight success. There are only those who dream big and seize their destinies. Focusing intentionally on an outcome is the power behind desire, and it leaves wishful thinking in the dust.

Channeling Your Desire

There's another Jeep! I can't believe it. They're everywhere!

Have you ever bought a new or used car and then noticed cars of the same make, model, and color cropping up everywhere? The fact is, they were there before. It wasn't your Google Home tracking your search history and surrounding you with live Jeep ads. What happened is your brain was thinking about it, so it noticed it. Simple as that. Once you bought the car, you started seeing it with frequency, convincing you it was everywhere. The world wasn't suddenly filled with more Jeeps. You just noticed and took note of them.

The name for this is the Baader-Meinhof[33] phenomenon. Also known as the "recency illusion"[34] or the "frequency illusion," it shows

---

[33] Staff, Pacific Standard. "There's a Name for That: The Baader-Meinhof Phenomenon." Pacific Standard, 14 June 2017, psmag.com/social-justice/theres-a-name-for-that-the-baader-meinhof-phenomenon-59670.
[34] "Language Log: Just between Dr. Language and I." Language Log, 7 Aug. 2005, itre.cis.upenn.edu/%7Emyl/languagelog/archives/002386.html.

us what it means to be human. It means that we notice what we think about. We notice more of what we are already noticing. We notice more than we think we do and understand far less.

This phenomenon is the reason we have confirmation bias. It's easy to confirm our beliefs and very difficult to overturn them. We don't like challenging our beliefs and thought patterns because our brain doesn't want to have to rewire itself. If we change our mind about big topics like religion, sex, or politics, we are painfully undoing wiring in our brains. It's partly why starting a new job, having a child, or getting really sick is so challenging, because you have to rewrite everything you do in order to accommodate the change.

What this phenomenon teaches us is dangerous and powerful—dangerous if we don't recognize it, and powerful if we use it to our advantage. If you can train your brain to focus on what YOU want, you'll start seeing solutions everywhere. You'll make connections between what you want and how to get it. You'll become a possibilist for your goals. You won't need to wait for bad things to happen, you can finally get dangerous by choosing your change before it chooses you.

Channeling desire means living like Tom Brady and becoming the embodiment of desire and effort. It means wanting something so bad that you work your tail off until you get it. It means figuring out your four points of purpose to live out your Ikigai.

Do you want your number-one goal badly enough? What's your motivation for living out your goal and purpose? It's hard to answer these questions as they cut to the root of motivation and how you structure your time, but it's important to consider your answers.

It's easier than you think to get started. Pick one focus goal and then get to work. Your goal will change and mold over time due to new learning and progress, but we all have to start somewhere.

The first step in creating an action plan is to pick one primary goal to focus on. You'll always have the busyness of life to contend with, and it doesn't mean you won't be able to watch your favorite show on Netflix. Your overarching goal will be the measure of daily success or failure.

So I ask again: What do you want most? What makes sense as your focus? What do you want to get out of this book?

Maybe you've done all the exercises up to this point, and you have a clear vision of your identity and how it fits into your purpose. Great! Now it's time to actually do something with it. Knowing is the first battle for your Destiny, but taking action and doing something about it is the all-important next step.

Action Step: What is your number-one heart's desire? How can you channel this desire into an actionable goal? And then, take the next step.

CHAPTER FIFTEEN: GET DANGEROUS WITH A 90-DAY PLAN

My wife and I were almost four years into our marriage when a deeper desire grew inside of us. Suddenly, we developed an otherworldly longing to see other places, live in a warmer climate, and take the next step to freedom. We both arrived at the same realization while together on a walk. Whether it was incredible timing or divine providence, we were thrilled but scared to take the next step.

It wasn't easy—when is life ever easy? Life sometimes gives you lemons, but most of the time, it gives you health complications, relational struggles, financial burdens, job problems, and various other challenges to overcome. The why was there, but leaving friends, finding new jobs, and figuring out the details seemed impossible.

How would we make it work? We had no ideas and no plan. We learned that taking that next step starts with knowing your why and having a direction, but if you aren't careful, the challenge of putting the plan in place can quickly overwhelm you.

I don't remember talking about our future together and what we really wanted earlier in our marriage. How weird is that? Maybe we were focused on other things in the honeymoon stage, but our walk, and subsequent thirst for more, kindled our desire to go beyond and live differently. We were extremely fortunate we were on the same page. We consider it divine intervention, and it helped us move forward and seek growth.

From that day forward, we started writing down our plans and checking in with our weekly goal progress. It felt invigorating to have a life goal we could work on together! All couples should experience the power of this type of goal setting, but don't worry if you aren't married or don't have a significant other. You need people around you to help you grow, but you can build the foundation for your plan on your own if needed.

Miranda and I had our why; now we just needed a strategy. Our plan several years ago was not as robust as the template built in this chapter, but the important thing is we wrote it down, worked on it, and stayed relentless. The 90-day plan here contains lessons learned from countless failures, tips for what actually works, and how to keep the plan alive and breathing.

90 Days to Reach Your Goal

90-day plans are the sweet spot. It's just enough to be doable and effective, but not so much that you lose interest or the resolve needed to complete your goal. You rarely know what you need until you start and you get your hands dirty. 90 days is the perfect time to practice, readjust, make errors, find success, and stay cognizant of the process.

Books like *Living Forward*[35] by Michael Hyatt and Daniel Harkavy and *Designing Your Life*[36] by Bill Burnett and Dave Evans are

---

[35] Hyatt, Michael, and Daniel Harkavy. Living Forward: A Proven Plan to Stop Drifting and Get the Life You Want. Illustrated, e-book, Baker Books, 2016.
[36] William Burnett (Consulting professor of design), et al. Designing Your Life. e-book, Alfred A. Knopf, 2016.

excellent resources for life planning. I've read them and recommend you do too. Create a life plan to have a major focus and a lens to make your decisions. But sometimes, getting caught up in the comprehensive process of planning your entire life will leave you feeling unsure of what to do next on a smaller scale. And if you're P on the MBTI? Watch out! Life planning will be even more challenging and difficult since you thrive off keeping your options open.

Focusing on the next 90 days simplifies everything. You don't need to have a 200-page life plan detailing every step in the life you want to live. Instead, you'll create a two to three-page action plan based on what you are learning in this book. Sounds much easier and more doable, right?

Yes, it's good to know exactly where you want to go, but you don't have to have it all figured out. Setting your compass heading and knowing the destination are pivotal to finding your way, but life rarely allows us to get what we want when we want it. Life is crazy and chaotic. Life is a joyous mess. If we get too caught up in a life plan, it will be hard to dodge the curve balls life inevitably throws at our heads.

So, read the aforementioned books and create a life plan, but start with a 90-day plan that focuses on your number-one goal. You'll find that everything falls into place much more quickly with this approach. It's a plan you can quickly complete and then get to work on right away. This matters. Action is the name of the game, and in this section, I will encourage you to take small action steps to learn and grow at the cost of having it all figured out in advance.

Another benefit of the 90-day plan is that you can adjust it over time AND see what you've done at the end. If you failed to reach your original goal by the end, you can see what you need to do differently over the next 90 days. No work is ever wasted as long as you use it to pivot to greater understanding and new directions. Don't go insane trying the same things repeatedly. Adjusting over time is how to win with life and 90-day plans.

The following chapters will show you how to make a 90-day action plan you can actually use. You'll learn how to channel your desire for your number one goal and turn it into action. I've made so many mistakes in my life, but I've learned from those errors and missteps. It's time for you to learn from my mistakes and hopefully avoid too many of your own. While the journey to your goal will be bumpy and filled with challenges, this section is here to remove a few of the speed bumps you might face along the way.

Create Your Personalized 90-Day Plan

A well thought out, written 90-day plan is the best way to get things done and move forward towards your Ikigai. Nothing beats planning and focusing on your number-one goal. It gives you the power of a singular focus, helps you track progress, directs your desire, and shows you where you're going.

An effective 90-day plan has five major features, each of which we'll discuss in this chapter:

1. One major goal
2. Purpose statement
3. Tasks
4. Positive habits to keep doing
5. Required resources
6. Weekly Review of goal and progress

As you progress through this chapter and this section, be mindful of what your 90-day plan will look like, and build it out. The action step for this chapter will direct you to a resource template you can use to get started if you prefer not to build it from scratch. Or, see the back of the book.

1) One Major Goal/Focus

You learned in the previous chapter about the power of having a singular focus. This doesn't mean you won't have other goals and things to do. Quite the contrary. We all have multiple goals, responsibilities, and things we want to do. Life is crazy, but that's the norm, and we have to deal with it. It's important to focus on the right goal and the right problem in order to make progress. If you spend all your time putting out fires, you won't be able to forge ahead on what matters most.

In the aforementioned book, *Designing Your Life,* the authors stress the importance of picking the right problem from the get-go:

> *It has been our experience, in office hour after office hour, that people waste a lot of time working on the wrong problem. If they are lucky, they will fail miserably quickly and get forced by circumstance into working on better problems. If they are unlucky and smart, they'll succeed—we call it the success disaster—and wake up ten years later wondering how the hell they got to wherever they are, and why they are so unhappy.*

Focus on the desire you want to fulfil that fits each of the four points of purpose. Spend a few days (a week at most) deliberating on your primary goal and then jump in. You'll learn more by taking the whirlwind of life head-on than deliberating ad nauseam. Decide to do something or not. It's now, at a specified time later, or not at all.

It's never someday. Someday never happens. Someday is a lie we tell ourselves to make ourselves feel better in the moment. You will never fulfil the plans you have to do something someday.

Focusing on one goal shouldn't come at the exclusion of all else. Historically, I struggle with this, as my number one goal often crowds out the rest of my life. But recently I've gotten much better with balance. So this focus comes at a cost, but it's one I'm willing to pay. Yes, you might have to wait several days for an email reply from me for a non-urgent matter, but I'm someone who gets things done. I choose relentless action over having everything neat and tidy.

SMART Goals

Do you know the SMART goal system? Now that you understand how to set the right goal from a big-picture perspective, let's run the goal through a few more checks and balances to optimize it. The SMART goal system is a handy way to check that your goal will work for you and not against you. I've seen far too many people set goals that are impossible to reach and track progress. Have you ever set a goal that's impossible to reach or track progress? The SMART system will help you avoid this pitfall. It's not the end-all-be-all of goal setting, but it's a valuable mindset.

S: Specific: The goal should match and move you forward specifically toward your current purpose, or relate to finding your purpose and determining great goals.

M: Measurable: At the end of the 90 days, goal completion or failure needs to be obvious.

A: Attainable: Is it possible to complete the goal in the next 90 days? Don't sell yourself short and dream small, but don't reach for the stars either if you haven't built the rocket ship yet.

R: Relevant: Does the goal relate to your purpose and what you're learning about yourself?

T: Time-bound: You got this one covered; it's a 90-day goal.

An example of a SMART goal is as follows.

Over the next 90 days, I will finish reading ten books and take three online courses related to my purpose. I'll accomplish this by spending the first week creating the book list and enrolling in relevant courses. I'll take thirty minutes out of each day to work toward this project. At the end, I will summarize my learning and create my next 90-day plan.

If you don't like the SMART goal system, that's fine. Here is a simplified version that works just as well. Make sure your goal passes two basic tests. Will it move you forward on your purpose? Are you excited to work on it? Figure out everything else as you go:

A few last notes on picking the right number-one goal:

- A great goal can be selfish, at least at first. We have to work on ourselves before we can give back. For example, losing weight so that you can live longer and have a greater impact is an excellent goal.
- Your goal can be to determine your purpose OR to accomplish something to better understand your purpose. If your goal is to read X amount of personal-growth books by the end of the 90 days, this is fine. Make sure it's measurable in terms of goal completion and your likelihood to complete, but even if by the end you still don't know what your ultimate purpose is, that's okay. We're all still learning.

- What do you think of your goal? Is it what you want to do for the next 90 days? Even though feedback is usually helpful, you get the final say in what you want to reach for. Go with your gut. It won't be a picnic, but it shouldn't be dinner alone with your in-laws either.
- Don't let fear block progress. Your goal won't be perfect, and it won't be exactly right. The power of living out your purpose is in the many iterations you'll make during the journey. It's the journey that counts, so buckle up and get started.

2) Purpose Statement

Write a brief statement in your plan that explains why your goal is important to you. This short sentence or two will serve as a reminder to you about why your goal is important to strive for over the next 90 days. If your goal is to lose weight, your purpose statement could be:

I want to lose weight so that I can do the things I want to do and live a long and healthy life. Losing weight will help me determine what it is I am meant to do by giving me the time and the clarity I need to do the work.

If your goal is to quit your job, your purpose statement might be:

I want to quit my job because it makes me unhappy and doesn't enable me to fulfill my purpose daily.

This is unique to you, and no one else needs to see it, so write whatever will motivate and remind you to keep moving forward even when it gets hard.

As Friedrich Nietzsche once said, *"If you know the 'why', you can live any 'how'."*

3) Tasks

A great 90-day plan will list the major action steps and tasks you need to do to complete the goal. While the main goal is something you want to measure such as losing a specific amount of weight, selling a certain amount of items in your online store, or having a better idea of what your purpose is by reading X amount of books, the tasks associated should be practical in nature.

Tasks include anything you need to do to move the goal forward. Think of ideas off the top of your head. You'll find you usually know the next steps. Even better, think about your goal constantly, and add good ideas when you get them.

The question of what to do for tasks is one that most books miss. Authors often share that we should have tasks related to our goals, but how do we know if the tasks are the right ones for the job? I've got you covered here. For goals, use the acronym SMART to make sure they meet the standard. For tasks, use the acronym FADOS:

F: Fit: Make sure selected tasks fit your skill set, and you can't delegate to others.

A: Apply: Connect the task to the SMART Goal. Make sure your tasks apply to your goals (it's easier than you might think to create a task list filled with items that have nothing to do with your primary goal. I do it all the time, and it's only on a second look that I catch this error!).

D: Doable: Each task should be completable by you without having to wait on someone else.

O: One-time tasks. Tasks you can cross off a list and get done. This isn't a list of habits you want to build or good things to keep doing. That's the fourth part of the 90-day plan.

S: Short: Tasks you can complete in under two hours. Break up anything taking more than two hours into separate tasks. Be thinking about the next specific step to get you closer to the goal.

Fill your task list with items that fit your skill set, apply to your goal, and are doable, one-time, quick tasks.

At the start, you won't know everything you need to do to complete your goal. To avoid being overwhelmed, start with a short list of ten tasks you know you can complete that fit the above criteria. You eventually won't need to use the above acronyms. Creating goals and tasks will become second nature, but do the hard work now so that you internalize it. As you get ideas, add them to a notebook, Trello board, or Evernote, and then continue to take action. Keep coming back to it and adjust as needed.

4) Positive Habits to Keep Doing

You'll notice that some ideas for tasks are more repeatable and harder to track. If you have an important task that you need to do every day, make a note of it. In my 90-day plans, I have a section called "positive habits to keep doing." It's not eloquent, but it's where I put the list of positive habits I want to continue that will help me have the energy to complete my primary goal. Prayer, fasting, reading, and healthy eating habits make the list here.

Building positive habits is hard, yet it's super easy. The smaller the habit, the easier the win. Positive habits are powerful forms of personal growth. They single-handedly provide the fuel necessary to achieve daily wins. It doesn't matter how small the win is. You create momentum when you achieve each small win, and this will give you the energy you need to achieve your 90-day goals.

The more positive habits in your life, the less room for negative habits and pitfalls. Positive habits are the most powerful way to avoid starting a negative habit. Focus on the positive elements of life and spend your time there. If you focus on the good, the bad won't have access to you. The more positive habits you build, the more enjoyable and productive life gets.

This is not to derail focus from the primary goal, but the best 90-day plan is realistic and flexible. You will have many other things in your life that you're doing other than working solely on your number-one goal. This section is here to help make the next 90 days the best three months of your life.

Make a short list of everything you're currently doing (or want to start doing) that helps keep you strong and full of momentum. This is my list for my most recent plan. Borrow items if it fits your plan.

- Regular running
- Practice intermittent fasting daily
- Nightly prayer and morning prayer on knees
- Develop better reading habits in the morning, such as **Hour of Power**
- Eating habits: less sugar, less soda, less alcohol, especially during the work week
- Painting, reading print books, meditating, anything not on screen
- Learning and practicing Portuguese
- Cooking and learning new recipes
- Look into joining Toastmasters
- Start church home group about spiritual gifts
- Up my coffee game. Elderberry lattes anyone?
- Do good things now so I can do great things later
- Give back to others and add value

5) Resources Needed

You don't know what you don't know.

This section is for planning the information you'll be taking in. It will help you be intentional about the content you'll be consuming over the next 90 days. It will give renewed energy to your reading and learning times, as the time you spend here will be in service of your larger goal. You won't have to wonder if the YouTube video, online course, book, or blog post is worth your time because you have planned it in advance. As soon as you finish, you can come back to your plan and update progress.

My previous plan included a list of books I read to provide the foundation for this book. It's important my writing is well-researched, and I know I don't have it all figured out. I want my final product to be great, and for that to happen, I need to read and reference books by people wiser than me.

My research list is all books. I listened to some books and read others on my Kindle. If you like videos and learn best with active instruction, make a list of video content you want to check out. Don't blast off into the YouTube black hole just yet, but make a note of which videos fit into your overall goal. Start with a Google search and branch out from there.

Since networking and building community is important, who do you need to talk to? For me, it's asking what authors and content creators I need to jump on a phone call with. If I can't talk directly to them, what resources of theirs can I pick up as the next best thing?

We won't succeed in a bubble. We need other people to help us along. Make a list of the people you want to talk to about your number-one goal over the next 90 days. When you speak to them, record notes from those conversations within your 90-day plan.

It should go without saying, but inform your spouse or significant other about your plan. If this is really important to you, they ought to know. Not just because it will help them understand, but the backing of our life partner can mean the difference between success or failure. Bring them on board. Make sure they know what you're up to.

6) Weekly Review and Action Plan for the Coming Week

The weekly review is the freshly baked bread and creamy butter of goal completion. It's how you get stuff done. It's unskippable and vital.

Working your tasks in weekly bursts allows you to put your head down and swim it out even when the seas are rough. For the week ahead, make a plan and then do those things. There's no deliberation during the week on what tasks are most important. You just do what you said you were going to do and get it done. As always, things will happen and emergencies might crop up, but the fundamental idea is to hustle and get to work during the week, avoiding second guessing whether the work you're doing is worth the time commitment. There's a time for planning and time for doing. Learn to find the flow for each.

When it comes time for the weekly review, do two things:

1. Review how the week before went. Did you get everything done? What needs to change? What updates do you need to make to your overall plan?
2. Plan the next week. Pick at least three items from your primary task list and plan to do these in the next week.

This weekly process will help your plan stay pliable and hold you accountable to finish important items. It's crucial for completing your goal to the best of your ability.

As you go, update your plan, and add any big change notes to the top, updated with the date. If you hit day 45 and things aren't looking good for goal completion, don't feel you need to stick your head in the sand and push forward no matter what. It might be exactly what you need to do, but if not, pivot and adjust your goal as needed.

Start right away, make a to-do list for the week based on your plan, and go for it. Give yourself grace; it's a process. You don't have to do it all right away and shouldn't. Prioritize anything that will depend on other people so that they have the time to complete it. When waiting on others, perform your time-consuming tasks first. Stay busy, but stay directed.

Create your plan, take small action steps, and finish reading.

Action Step: Download your 90-day action plan template or create your own. Join the free course for examples and links to download a template: https://www.jmring.com/cyd-book/

CHAPTER SIXTEEN: EMBRACE AN ACTION BIAS

I wear $30 barefoot-type shoes when I run. I don a shirt I received for free from a Camp Gladiator boot camp I used to attend. I use $10 headphones that are falling apart. I listen to audiobooks or music from my budget smartphone (also failing). I got my shorts for five euros at a used clothing store in Lisbon. My socks and underwear are the most expensive part of my ensemble because I don't skimp on the important things.

I am not an Olympic runner, nor would I wow you with my pace times. But running is a habit I cultivated and increased during the pandemic, and hope to continue. I love the feeling of the wind on my face, the heat that rises within me when I'm hitting a steady pace, and the runner's high at the end of it all. I also love eating a guilt-free cookie (or two or three…) after a healthy recovery dinner. I didn't need a ton of gear to start this habit, nor do I need fancy gadgets to continue. I just need basic equipment in order to keep up the habit and enjoy progress.

Whatever you want to do, whatever you want to change, whatever desire is bubbling to the surface, don't wait on fancy tools to get started. Goals and habits aren't equal. Skiing will be more expensive than running, but don't wait for the laptop you can't afford, the $200 running shoes that only increase blisters, or the acceptance letter from a higher education program. Don't wait when today is calling.

Waiting until you have everything set in place is not the best way to reach your goals. Waiting until you have the best tools doesn't work either. Optimizing over time is the better option. I don't like to admit I struggle in many areas of life, but my close friends will tell you I've mastered the action piece. No matter what the goal is, I'm off to the races before I've even considered all angles. I often leap before I even peek over the cliff. This is dangerous living, but it's the best way to succeed.

Take this quote from Pablo Picasso to heart:

"I am always doing that which I cannot do, in order that I may learn how to do it."

Life is full of risks, challenges, and painful outcomes. But this is true regardless of what you do. Hunkering down won't free you from the slow decay of life. Peter Drucker sums it up best:

"People who don't take risks generally make about two big mistakes a year. People who do take risks generally make about two big mistakes a year."

Leap before you look and embrace an action bias. The details don't matter, only the decision to go. Don't let the fear of what might happen stop you from going for broke. Don't feel like you have to be 100% ready to go before you take the leap. Make one small good decision right now, despite your current level of skill or basic equipment.

Live Dangerously and Embrace the Suck

The craziest thing I've ever done is moving away from the United States to travel the world indefinitely. As you learned in my story earlier, this didn't go as planned, but it still ranks as the most difficult thing I've ever done. It was hard saying goodbye to friends and family, and it was challenging to part with most of our material belongings, but we did it, and it was the right choice. The right choice is usually not the easy one. I wish I knew why this is the case.

What made this life-changing decision easier for us is that we decided long ago not to let fear of change stop us from moving forward. We unequivocally choose to live dangerously and without regret. We know that as soon as we choose comfort over pain, we'll lose progress and stymie growth. Despite the difficulty change presents, we know our potential is linked to the choice to move forward.

Embrace the suck by living dangerously. Take the time to make plans, but don't get stuck in planning mode. It's only when we get over the last wave that we find calmer waters. If we stick to the safety of what we know, we won't ever move forward. Get busy living the life you deserve to live.

Every tool, piece of advice, and story I've shared in this book is to get you moving forward with power and energy. But no tool, no course, no book, no coaching session, nor inspirational quote will help unless you decide to take action and change your life. Building a 90-day plan is worthless unless you decide to take action on your desire.

I have to exhaust this point, because 99% of people who want to do something different with their lives, don't. Most of the people who buy this book won't even get to this section. Most of these readers won't build their own 90-day action plan. I've known too many people who regret not doing more with their lives. I've heard from one too many older folks who wish they had tried X, done more of X, or spent more time with X.

Nobody regrets the risks they took. Everyone regrets the chances they didn't take.

I implore you to embrace your dangerous side and make crazy progress. Quit your job to pursue your business idea. Take a chance on you by throwing away (or giving away) every food item in your kitchen and starting from scratch with healthy ingredients. Go for broke and ask your crush out on a date, or renew your wedding vows with your spouse.

Go crazy. Be crazy. Live life as if there is no tomorrow. Stop living as if the purpose of life is to arrive safely at death. It's not. Life can be so much more than you're living right now, but you have to be ready to make it happen. Take the leap before you look and dive into the unknown.

Low-Cost Action Probes

I've saved the best strategy for right now. Ready for it? Start on your journey, whatever that journey is, by initiating low-cost action probes to test the waters. This way you can live dangerously and leap before you look, but it won't be life altering if you fall on your face. This is the "safe" and calculated way to move forward. You're still taking action, but you're now balancing that action with smart decisions.

Low-cost probes allow you to take the next step, whatever the next step is, in a safer and more manageable way. Start with a day pass at the gym, a salad for lunch, or replacing soda with water for losing weight. If you're intent on finding your dream job, Interview someone who has the job you want, intern at an agency with the job, or get a necessary certification now. If you want to take your business to the next level, make a phone call, show up to the next convention, create a new digital product to give away.

The key to maximizing success with low-cost probes is in the analysis. This entire strategy is to gather data. What worked? What didn't? What steps do you think will work for you? What tasks are you going to add to your 90-day plan? What tasks or goals do you need to change or remove?

As you've been learning, go with your strengths. Don't focus too much on what you are not going to do, but focus on doing more of what you are great at. Do more of the baby steps you know you need to take, but have been hesitating on. Take action right now and make progress using what you know about yourself. Use your newfound superpowers, strengths, and personality insights to forge ahead.

Use low-cost probes to cultivate a 90-day action plan to help you build the life you want.

Action Step: What's something you've always wanted to do but haven't? Go do it right now if possible, or plan a weekend trip. It doesn't matter if it's silly. What matters is taking action on something new and exciting.

CHAPTER SEVENTEEN: TWO TOOLS TO CRUSH YOUR 90-DAY PLAN

I've battled anxiety and depression off and on for the better part of my life, most of the time unknown to me. Sometimes I have it mastered and function well. Other times it hits me like a truck, and I don't even want to get out of bed in the morning. I know my feelings and brain functions are tied to different causes, some of which I can't control. What I eat, how much I exercise, how my author business is doing, what's going on in the world, and how connected I feel with the people and community around me contribute to the ebbs and flows of anxiety.

Add to this the frenzy and confusion of the coronavirus pandemic, and you have yourself a recipe for disaster. But with the power of intentional living and optimization, I've been fortunate to stay afloat and make sure I was using my time wisely.

I'm only starting on my path to learning more about the mind-body connection and the unsurprising fact that what we think and feel directly influences our physical bodies. If you believe you are healthy, you often are. If you fear pain and spend your life worrying, that pain will manifest in your body. We are what we think. The ancient Chinese Philosopher Lao Tzu once said:

"Watch your thoughts, they become your words; watch your words, they become your actions; watch your actions, they become your habits; watch

your habits, they become your character; watch your character, it becomes your destiny.”

The secret is twofold: intentional living, and learning how to pivot with power. Intentional living is the driving force behind leaving anxiety and depression in the dust. If I plan my day the night before, I'm much more apt to have a successful, productive, influential, and otherwise happy day. If I wake up with a sense of daily purpose and a clear sense of how to live that out, I'm much better off.

Pivoting with power means recognizing where you are going wrong and righting the ship before hitting the iceberg. It's one of the most important tools in the Destiny seeker's arsenal, but it's also the most difficult to master.

The what is important, but the how is even more critical. I want you to close this book not just with knowledge or motivation, but with a bias towards positive action. I want you to know what you need to do next and avoid overwhelm. It's impossible to give a one-size-fits-all prescription for how to do anything, but each step along the way creates progress. This book's goals are lofty, so let's take a stab at becoming people of intentionality.

Intentional Living and Optimization

There is nothing better than a good ol' burst of intentionality to get you over the hump. Yes, this might seem like just another personal growth tactic, but I've included it here because intentional living is the countermove to regret. Learn to live with intentionality and focused thought and you will never regret another thing in your life.

In his book *Intentional Living*,[37] John C. Maxwell shares:

> *When you live each day with intentionality, there's almost no limit to what you can do. You can transform yourself, your family, your community, and your nation. When enough people do that, they can change the world. When you intentionally use your everyday life to bring about positive change in the lives of others, you begin to live a life that matters.*

Taking bold action requires a shift in how you operate. It means moving from how you used to do things and trying alternative approaches. I'm nowhere near complete on the road to optimizing my life. I won't ever reach 100% optimization because of the convoluted nature of life. But intentional living and setting goals and tasks for the week ahead serve the purpose of achieving those goals, despite anything life throws my way.

You can optimize your life with a weekly planning approach. As noted as part of a great 90-day plan, weekly planning is the bread and butter to living out your purpose and actually getting things done. Write down three to five of the most important tasks for the week ahead using the 90-day plan framework and attack those tasks with absolute fury. Let nothing get in the way. Suffer whatever consequences come your way for other tasks, and fight to get done what matters most.

As you go forward, you will suffer trials and setbacks. You might get to day 30 of your 90-day plan and feel you have no hope of accomplishing your goal. But this is never the case. Progress follows the struggle. The challenging times we face move us forward in strength and infuse our actions with purpose.

---

[37] Maxwell, John C. Intentional Living: Choosing a Life That Matters. Reprint, e-book, Center Street, 2017.

I had one of my more mature thoughts the other day. I'm not holding my breath for more, but here it is: It started with the normal, "I wish this situation were easier. I'm so tired of the struggle." Then it ended with a profound realization. I thought:

Do I really want it to be easier? Isn't it the struggle that is creating strength and fostering insight? If I didn't go through this, I wouldn't be armed with the knowledge, patience, and ability to optimize for next time. I wouldn't be nearly as strong moving forward if I didn't have to deal with the mess before me. If I made it through this time without the struggle, wouldn't it just make next time much harder?

I don't want to deal with pain. Neither do you. But often, the very thing we hope to avoid is exactly what we need to go through to optimize our situation. Be intentional about staying true to the course and continuing the struggle, even if it seems hopeless or overwhelming. There is always light at the end of the tunnel.

Set your intention by year, 90 days, month, week, and by day. Go by year with big goals you want to accomplish. Set it by month by looking at what you can accomplish this month if everything goes right. Plan the week based on new knowledge and what's actually happening in your life. Plan to attack each day with a goal, even if what you need that day is a day off from thinking about the plan! And, of course, keep working on your 90-day plan.

What intentional living is:

- Choosing your activities and actions. You're in the driver's seat of your life. Don't sit at the back.
- Knowing your specific plan for the next hour, day, and week.
- Having a broad plan for the next month, 90 days, and year.

- Making major life decisions through the lens of your identity and purpose.
- Battling through your struggles and embracing overwhelm.
- Building your environment around your goals.
- Understanding to your core why you get up every day. Knowing your why.

What intentional living isn't:

- Scrolling through your phone for no reason.
- Following a rigid schedule and being limited by unrealistic expectations.
- Getting to day 30 of the 90-day plan, realizing you can't make it, and then quitting instead of adapting.
- Planning for every eventuality and being fearful of every terrible outcome.
- Hustling and squeezing out every drop of productivity from your life.
- Living with a sense of overwhelm and lack of purpose.
- Finding yourself repeatedly in an environment not suited to making progress.
- Sacrificing important moments and milestones for the sake of progress.

Living with intention and purpose is the opposite of living in the past. Envision your future and what you want to become, and do the steps necessary to get there. Don't beat yourself up if you miss a step. Keep moving forward in strength and commitment to your purpose. Optimize as you get to know yourself and practice your purpose. You will learn so much just by moving forward and taking a big life step.

Be intentional by living with a ferocious desire to accomplish your number-one goal. Channel the desire into solid action. Take stock and pivot as needed. Jump into the next thing before you are ready, but not before you make a plan. Plan to win big but don't let failure keep you down. Live with intention and optimization.

Pivot with Power

Pivoting is a tricky business. The last thing you want is to switch paths the moment before you strike gold. Knowing when to make the call to pivot in a new direction is one of the most challenging goals we will tackle in this book. I want to handle it with care because sometimes all you need to do is push one more step forward. Other times, the best thing would be to cut your losses and make a brand-new plan.

From my personal experiences, and in coaching others, I've found that it's always worth it to give the 90 days everything you have. Dive into a singular goal. It's worth the push vs. the continuous and easier route of switching plans and going for something new. Goals and progress have a nasty habit of taking twice as long as you think and three times as long as you'd like.

Some people will dive in and refuse to pivot when it's obvious they should, while other people can't last seven days into a 90-day plan. Be prepared to bleed a little. You build muscle by tearing it down. Give it more than you think it needs and more than you think you can.

Pivoting with Power means taking a step back and evaluating current progress and how far you have left to go. And then, and only then, tweaking your existing plan. Pivoting with power means quickly righting the ship and surging ahead, even if the sails are still only halfway up. Remember, having a bias to action is the key.

It's okay if you need to pivot on day 30 of the action plan because you've made no progress, but you don't need to start over completely. Save time and progress and modify your plan instead. This will allow you to find the right level of success, and to start fresh on your next plan, instead of working on your first past the original 90 days. Nothing says you can't update your number-one goal as you go. In fact, I encourage this if it's needed to keep you going.

Sometimes pivoting means asking for feedback or advice on how to move forward. Most of the time, you know in your gut which decision is right. If you still aren't sure whether to pivot or surge forward, consider these questions:

1. Is your goal long-term and going to take time? Some goals just take longer than others to come to fruition. If there's one thing I've learned, it's that sometimes taking a step back breeds incredible results.

2. What other people have had similar goals to yours? What did they do to reach their goals? What was their timetable like? You'll never be able to repeat success in the same way, but if you are way off the mark, it might mean recalculating your action steps.

3. Do you love what you're doing? Fulfilling your purpose and attaining your 90-days goal will not always be rainbows and butterflies, but it should be enjoyable most of the time. If you get frustrated and quickly burnt out, it could be a red flag that you need to make a shift.

4. Are you suffering from loss aversion? Loss aversion is the principle of feeling a loss more than a gain. Are you feeling the pain of lost time or are unsure if your current progress is worth all this trouble? Does it feel like you are getting nowhere? Go back to your why and channel your desire.

The first leg of the race is the toughest, so struggle through and look forward to gains later on.

Pivoting with power involves not losing ground. It means moving forward with intention and a new direction, using what you've learned about yourself along the way. Analyze how far you've come. See what works. Throw in the towel on bad ideas and invest heavily in what's working. This is the unique advantage of reaching any goal: pivoting when needed and infusing that pivot moment with the wealth of knowledge you've already earned by taking action.

Action leads to learning. Learning either leads to goal completion or "failure." Failure becomes the catalyst for change, and you come back stronger than ever. Because living out your purpose is an iterative process, you'll eventually build a 90-day plan that, when living it out, exceeds your wildest expectations.

Your advantage is the ability to use failure points to blast forward. Use what works and what doesn't to live out your best life. Track everything and always take action. Pivot with power when needed and soar.

Action Step: What's one productivity tool you know works for you, but you've been ignoring recently? Make an action statement below with your commitment to using it this week.

_____

_____

_____

CHAPTER EIGHTEEN: OVERCOMING THE WHIRLWIND OF LIFE

Vacuuming the dining room because dinner ran late and my servers needed to get home to do their homework... Getting food stains all over my nice new teal blue shirt because I had to run the dishwasher during dinner service... Taking a walk-in tour at eight PM just when I was getting ready to take a quick break... All on the same night... Oh, and did I mention this wasn't just one time, but a frequent occurrence? Yikes. The whirlwind of life was on full display and threatening to knock me back. Retiring at 27 sounded like fun... Right? Wrong.

Serving and loving our residents meant being there for them when they needed us and giving our best to ensure the highest quality of living. My time was not mine to dictate. I gave up control to serve. I was okay with this. It was a humbling experience.

I knew going into my stint as a manager at a retirement community that the work would have late nights, 60-hour work weeks, overnight on-calls, and availability during our "off" days. My wife, Miranda, and I worked together, which was amazing, but we worked all the time. And by the end of the two years we were exhausted. The whirlwind of life had us on the ropes, and it was all we could do to survive and keep going.

But you know what? Survive we did. During this two-year stint, I wrote three books, stayed fit and healthy, and achieved several life goals. I don't say this to brag (you should know me better by now), but to share that no matter how busy life gets, there's no excuse for not completing your most important goals. I don't miss the whirlwind by any means, but it was great training. The whirlwind has a nasty habit of creeping in, and before you know it, you fill your week with tasks that don't really matter and don't move you forward on your goals.

Once you're clear on your purpose, there's no reason not to do what you said you wanted to do. Once you're filled with desire, nothing can keep you from living out your purpose. Knowing yourself better, understanding your purpose, and creating a plan to live out your best, is what works. It's a push to focus solely on what matters most. And that's how you beat the whirlwind.

In his book, *The Bullet Journal Method*,[38] Ryder Carroll says:

"Inevitably, we find ourselves tackling too many things at the same time; spreading our focus so thin that nothing gets the attention it deserves. This is commonly referred to as "being busy." Being busy, however, is not the same thing as being productive."

Busyness is a poor excuse for not getting something important done. We all have time for whatever we deem important. There are twenty-four hours in each day, and even if you have a full-time job, a big family, and other competing interests and responsibilities, you're not maxed out, even if you feel like you are. No one is so busy that they can't step back and take a few minutes of positive action, which will compound over time. Five minutes may not seem like much for one day, but 35 minutes over the course of a week will help you resurface and make progress.

---

[38] Carroll, Ryder. The Bullet Journal Method: Track the Past, Order the Present, Design the Future. Illustrated, Portfolio, 2018.

And I hear you busy parents, college students with tons of homework, and young professionals. I know life can be crazy. But I'll say again: We make time for what's important.

What parent, if their child needed to chat about something serious, wouldn't make time for them? What college student wouldn't make time to go out on a date with their crush if asked? What busy young professional would say no to a Friday night game of ping-pong with a side of BBQ chicken wings?

If you keep finding yourself behind or not completing your goals, you haven't prioritized them. You need to choose whether you're going to accomplish something. Choosing not to do it is okay and even encouraged. Lingering to-do list items you want to do eventually but that don't match your number-one priority are just weighing you down. Put these whirlwind items on another list and save them for later.

Keep Your To-Do List Clean

You can choose to put something off when life gets crazy. Sometimes, life can get suddenly overwhelming, and it's all you can do to keep your head above water for a few weeks. But ask yourself: Am I dealing with a one-off circumstance, or is my life always this busy?

If you're always running around like a chicken with your head cut off, stop and take a breath. You're not meant to live at such a chaotic pace. You don't have to live like this. You have permission to take a second for YOU and get your life back on track. Everyone else in your life will benefit from it.

The first step is to cut unnecessary events, time-sucking commitments, and other activities that aren't directly related to your most important goals. In his book *The Ruthless Elimination of Hurry*,[39] John Mark Comer says:

"Our time is our life, and our attention is the doorway to our hearts."

We have to get it right. We don't get to live our lives again. Our time here on Earth is our one shot at making it count. Make time for what's important, and you'll live life with no regrets. Look at your current to-do list. Clear and cut ruthlessly. You don't have time for everything. Remove items you really want to get to, but know it's not likely you'll be able to complete this week.

I keep my to-do list on a Trello board. It saves me a ton of time and helps keep my life digitally organized. When I look ahead to the week and have over ten things on my list, I regularly clean house. This means moving to-do list items into a separate board for safekeeping. It gives me the peace of mind knowing the idea isn't gone but saved into a "not-right-now" list. If you're like me, you have more ideas than you know what to do with. This is fantastic for brainstorming, but will slow you down if you don't learn to sort and prioritize.

Make sure your list of to-dos only includes items that pass the FADOS test. Make sure your tasks relate to what you most want to accomplish. There's no need to put "take the trash out" or "do the dishes" on a to-do list. These things will either get done, or they won't. Don't bog your list down with items that won't impact your most important goal. And better yet, if the item on your to-do-list takes less than five minutes to complete, do it now, don't wait!

---

[39] Comer, John Mark, and John Ortberg. The Ruthless Elimination of Hurry: How to Stay Emotionally Healthy and Spiritually Alive in the Chaos of the Modern World. e-book, WaterBrook, 2019.

Make time for what's most important by ruthlessly cutting out activities that don't serve your end goal.

You Don't Need More Time—You Need Clearer Priorities

More time isn't what you need. It's what we think we need, but it isn't the actual issue. You won't believe me until you experience it, but let me try anyway. When's the last time you were productive on a vacation? Every day I spent working at the retirement community meant one more day of not working on my goals. But you better believe that when our off days came around, I was clambering to get out my laptop and get to work.

A relentless pursuit of your goals is still possible, even during a busy season of life.

More time is what I thought I needed back in the day, but what was driving my success and my get-it-done attitude was the time crunch. Parkinson's law[40] agrees with me here. The term, first coined by Cyril Northcote Parkinson, states that work expands to the time allotted. I had to fit my primary goals into my off time, so I did. When I first expanded into full-time entrepreneurship, I wasn't nearly as productive as I was when I only had a few hours to do the work. It's a conundrum with major implications to our pursuit of Destiny.

I thought that having all the time in the world would benefit me (and it did in some ways), but my productivity didn't go through the roof as I expected. Instead, I would have been better off setting 90-day goals rather than naively assuming that since the world was now my oyster, I could create pearls.

---

[40] The Economist. "Parkinson's Law." The Economist, 10 July 2020, www.economist.com/news/1955/11/19/parkinsons-law.

The Urgent Will Always Be There (and It's Not Really Urgent Anyway...)

The urgent tasks will never go away. You must learn to face this reality head-on, handle it quickly, and be okay with ignoring the tasks outright if you're in focus mode.

Obviously, there are different levels of urgency for tasks. Answering a GIF text from your friend isn't urgent, but an actual fire raging in your kitchen is. Urgency isn't normally obvious. It's never this easy. You have to make a choice between several tasks, all competing for your attention. Even at the best of times, this can be confusing and feel impossible.

But it's not impossible. You can implement reasonable systems to minimize distractions and spend ample time on work that matters. The key is being clear on what is urgent for you and then tackling those urgent matters quickly and efficiently. Start by setting your phone to do-not-disturb except for calls from your spouse, your boss, or other emergencies.

When I'm in focused writing mode, I need minimal distractions, so I turn my phone on do-not-disturb, turn it off, or I set it aside. This doesn't always stop me from going to it to distract myself, but if someone tries to call or text me, chances are good that I'll miss it. If I'm in writing mode or doing other work that requires intense focus, I don't answer.

The urgent is always there, but it's most likely not that urgent. Make time and space for people to contact you if they REALLY need to, but otherwise you owe it to yourself and your productivity to turn down your availability in order to produce. Entrepreneur extraordinaire and online business guru Tim Ferriss said:

Develop the habit of letting small bad things happen. If you don't, you'll never find time for the life-changing big things.

Don't be afraid of the whirlwind crashing about you. Sometimes you need to let the waves hit you to come out the other side stronger with your goals complete.

Make Your 90-Day Plan a Living, Breathing Document

Another key part of overcoming the whirlwind and focusing on your number-one goal is to keep it front and center. Make your 90-day plan a living, breathing document. Either print it out and keep it with you at all times or keep it up as a tab on your browser. This will keep you motivated and force you to keep thinking of it, updating it, and setting weekly tasks that relate to what you want to get done.

Make time to check in every week with yourself about your plan. Setting yourself up for a successful week is the big-ticket way to get things done. Do this one thing, and I almost guarantee success with your goals. You don't have to think too hard on this. All you need do is pick a time on Sunday afternoon and check your goals and set your most important tasks for the coming week.

This is most successfully done with an accountability partner, but you can do this on your own too. Using your 90-day plan as the guidepost, choose the most important tasks you will accomplish this week. Don't write that you have to pick up the laundry on Tuesday or that date night is Friday. You can do these things during the week, but don't add them to your weekly task list here. This list is sacred! Only put the tasks here that matter the most and directly relate to your primary goals.

At the end of every week, plan your next week ahead to crush your goals. Use the power of the weekly review to keep the 90-day plan front and center. Come back to it often by updating it, keeping it open as a tab, or making a daily to-do list item to review it. The whirlwind will bury it if you let it. Keep the dragon at bay by focusing any extra energy you possess on your 90-day plan. Live it. Breathe it. Keep it front and center.

Maximize Your Best Time of Day

Most gurus out there will tell you to wake up at the crack of dawn and do your most important tasks first. I don't agree.

We need to work at the time of day we do our best work. We need to take action when it makes the most sense for us to do so.

If you are a night owl, work on your goals at night. Morning person? Wake up early. Do your best work on a Sunday afternoon when everyone else is napping or watching football? Crush it then.

I do my best work at night and thus, since my main goals are writing related, I plan my weekly schedule to include late afternoon and evening times for writing. Don't get locked into the mentality of following a system that doesn't work for you. Experiment and find your best time and do your work then. Find what works for you and then actually do it.

How to Create Time: Ten Tactics for Building Margin

If you've mastered your priorities and are still struggling to find the time to get things done, I got you. These tactics will get you started on the right foot.

As you reach the end of this book, combine these tips with what you are learning about yourself and what you already know to be true.

Knowing you're an unorganized or inconsistent person is beneficial in the quest to find more time to get things done. Know your struggles and use your strengths to overcome them.

My bottom-tiered theme on the CliftonStrengths Finders is consistency. I know that trying to do things every single day will be a struggle. I've embraced this part of me, and I don't kick myself if I don't keep a regular writing habit, even though writing every day is the most-often touted tip to becoming a successful writer. I've had much more success scheduling out longer writing sessions a few times per week than typing 1000 words per day.

The key to creating time and completing your number-one goal is to do what works for you. This is not cop-out advice, it's getting to know yourself at a deeper level and then moving forward in this knowledge. It's not an excuse to fail; it's living with intentionality so that you do the best work you can do.

Here are ten tactics for building margin into your life for working on the most important:

1) Get organized. Get physically, digitally, and mentally organized. Clutter on your desk and workspace can lead to lost time. Too many items on your computer desktop will create chaos and lost files. A busy mind can't focus on what you need to do right now with too many thoughts floating around.

2) Don't set yourself up for failure. Choose two or three important tasks for the week ahead and hold yourself accountable for task completion. Keep it simple, but keep moving forward.

3) Get up an hour earlier or stay up an hour later. Don't sacrifice sleep over the long-term, but if you need a bit of extra time to get the job done, don't be afraid to do it.

4) Practice intentionality. Schedule time for specific task completion. I write on Sunday afternoons, every Sunday afternoon. It's sacred time, and I make the most of it by sometimes writing well into the evening after I get in the flow.

5) Avoid time wasters. Watching an episode of your favorite reality TV show is perfectly fine, but after two or three episodes, catch yourself. Try not to rationalize activities that don't fit into your overall purpose.

> *Whenever I'm about to do something, I think, "Would an idiot do that?" And if they would, I do not do that thing. —Dwight Schrute, The Office.*

6) Listen to an audiobook that directly relates to your number-one goal while walking, cleaning, cooking, or driving. Multitasking isn't always the best idea, but be smart about it and do it when it makes sense.

7) Practice the art of saying no. You do not have time for every opportunity that comes your way. This is painfully true once your purpose becomes clear. You'll get requests for many activities that don't relate to your goals. Now that you know what you need to do, you'll find the world suddenly wants to pull you in a million different directions. Resist the pull. No need to say no to everything, but be highly selective with your time. Use your priorities as a guide.

8) Work without distractions. You'll get a lot more done if you put your phone on silent mode, check emails only twice per day, and schedule time for distracting activities vs. allowing random interruptions.

9) Learn what tasks require greater attention and prioritize those tasks. Sometimes it's okay to talk to others and be distracted. Not all

tasks are the same. Learn what needs your absolute focus and attention to give your best.

10) Use social media as you would a screwdriver. Use it sparingly and wisely but otherwise keep it in the kitchen junk drawer.

Live your best life by creating time for your number-one goal and get to it.

It's Mindset, and It's Not

It's not fair to end our discussion about the whirlwind here. I want to recognize and confirm this step isn't easy. In fact, it's one of the most difficult aspects of getting things done and moving forward on your 90-day plan. How do you make progress toward a big goal when life is already so ridiculously overwhelming?

Busyness is a mindset. I firmly believe we all have more time than we realize. It's why we've discussed the importance of a time audit and knowing what you do with your time. It might surprise you how much wiggle room you have. There are hidden minutes you could put to good use, you need only find them.

But just as important is that life is tough. It rarely throws us a bone, it usually throws us curve balls and problems. You need only consider the entire year of 2020 for a few seconds to realize that life is messy and unpredictable. Your goals are important, and Catalyzing your Destiny is a great venture, but it should never come at the cost of not enjoying the present moment and appreciating all that you have.

There is such a fine line here. I can't in good conscience tell you to take it one day at a time and hope that you complete your goals. Far too many people get to the end of their lives filled with regret because they took it one day at a time. The balance here is yours to strike. But I urge you, no I *admonish* you, to find the time every single week to move toward your goals. Enjoy life, yes, but make time for what's most important.

Action Step: What is the biggest contributor to your personal whirlwind? Name one way you might overcome.

_____

_____

_____

CONCLUSION: PUTTING THE PIECES OF YOUR LIFE PURPOSE PUZZLE TOGETHER

I recently took up oil painting as a new hobby. You won't see my works on your Facebook feed anytime soon, but I'm enjoying it. My mother and my mother-in-law both loved the Christmas tree painting I shared over Christmas, so that's a win.

I paint to give my intuitive futuristic mind a break from thinking deeply to be in the moment and enjoy using my senses. It's also not a task requiring a computer or phone screen, which is a huge plus. It's fun, but it's also a monumental struggle as I aim to take the time and care necessary to bring my vision to life. It's so different from anything else I do, and it's great.

I recently finished up a painting of the moon. It's not bad at all for a first-time attempt. The part that took the longest wasn't putting the framework down. It was the fine details, blending, and finishing touches that took hours upon hours of fine-tuning to get right. Just like a painting, you are a work in progress. Fine-tuning your personality, understanding your purpose, and taking action are not easy things to do. Nothing about taking your life to the next level is easy.

View your growth as an iterative process. You don't have to meet all your goals to be successful. You don't have to absolutely crush your first 90-day plan. You don't have to unlock your purpose just from reading a book or by taking an online course. All you have to do is move forward. To keep breathing. To take stock of your current circumstance in its entirety and keep going.

With this mindset, every step you take towards living out your purpose is positive, even if you fall flat on your face. Even if the outcome of the next step feels like two steps back, it isn't. As long as you are taking positive action and weighing your next steps against your identity and your current purpose, you can't lose! This should feel freeing. You can't go wrong as long as you move forward to the best of your ability with what you know.

It's not easy at all, but it is.

I'm guilty of putting far too much pressure on myself and trying to maximize my potential so much that it becomes painful. It's only by merging what I know about myself into every step forward that I've been able to see steady growth. The way forward is to get your hands dirty, your feet tired, and your travel bag packed.

Your Life-Purpose Puzzle: Putting it Together

Self-discovery tools are the pieces on the outside edges of your life puzzle. With these in place, you can much more easily know where the inside pieces go, even if you don't have the full picture. These form the foundation of what is possible for you.

It's MUCH easier to start here because you can base important life decisions on whether they match the outside edges. Despite the analogy, life is NEVER like a real puzzle. Instead, in order to complete your personal puzzle, you have to contend with thousands of other pieces that might look right at first glance but are actually part of another puzzle entirely. Find just the right pieces and use only those.

The Ikigai forms the rest of your puzzle pieces. Use it to sort out which pieces will fit the edge pieces and then fill in the rest with what makes sense to be there. It has to match. Your Ikigai has to match what you actually are or what you can reach. It doesn't do any good if it doesn't match the edge pieces of your identity.

And finally, the 90-day action plan is the process of putting the puzzle together with your hands, one piece at a time. Without snapping the pieces together, the puzzle will never come together. Action is the lifeblood of any good plan. Without a bias towards taking small action steps, your life will look like a puzzle after a toddler meltdown: incomplete, messy, and with missing pieces.

I don't have a magic formula. This analogy is as close as I can get. I wish I could snap my fingers and share exactly what your purpose in life is, but it doesn't work like that. And you don't want it to. You don't want me or anyone else to tell you what your Destiny is. Decide for yourself what you want to do with your life. It takes hard work, grit, and a relentless ability to move forward despite setbacks.

Armed with self-discovery tools and a passion for finding out who you are, your identity lies within reach. With the Ikigai, you have a much better idea of what's actually possible for you. With your 90-day action plan in place, you can go forward with intentional action and take the road to incredible progress.

I've laid out the path before you to Catalyze your Destiny. And just like the story of Bronco from the foreword, I've invited you to the party. Now I urge you to get started before it's too late. We will never have a guarantee of how much time we have left. As of this writing, there are no special pills to grant immortality, nor is there any way to prevent accidents from occurring. Nothing is certain and guaranteed. Your decision today impacts the rest of your life.

18 Takeaways to Catalyze Your Destiny

Before you close out this book, I have 18 takeaways for you. Don't worry, I'll make them brief. Come back here often if you need a source of inspiration to go get your life goals and live your purpose.

1. **Internalize and harness your uniqueness.** You are the one and only you. Live YOUR life, not someone else's.
2. **Choose pain over comfort.** Try new things and live dangerously.
3. **Develop a questioning habit.** Question why you do the things you do. Question your beliefs. Question your routine. Question your habits.
4. **Details don't matter.** You'll figure out the details as you go. Don't let details stop you from moving forward.
5. **Embrace the suck.** Things are never as easy as they should be, or as easy as you want them to be. Choose what's hard and challenging over what's easy.
6. **Overnight successes don't exist.** It will always take you longer than you want to reach your goals.
7. **Keep learning about *you*.** You're ever-changing, unique, and just plain wonderful.
8. **Optimize with intentionality.** Set your intention for the day, week, month, and years ahead for long-term success.
9. **Pivot with power.** Be ready to pivot when needed, but do so with intentionality and careful consideration based on what you know about yourself.
10. **Focus on your strengths.** Do what you're good at. Don't dwell on your weaknesses.
11. **Be SMART and use FADOS.** Make SMART goals and FADOS tasks to succeed.
12. **Catalyze your Destiny with desire.** Desire for your goal is the best way to find success no matter how long you take or how tough the journey forward is.

13. **Get your priorities straight**. Create time by remembering what's most important and filtering decisions through this lens. Be clear about what you actually spend your time on, and shift as needed.

14. **Avoid getting sucked up by the whirlwind of life.** Use the strategies you've learned in this book to focus on what's most important to you.

15. **Chase your Ikigai.** Run toward your Ikigai and the life of your dreams. Keep chasing it until you find it.

16. **Make a 90-day plan**: Create a unique 90-day plan that you are excited about and want to complete.

17. **Develop an action bias**: Whenever you get stuck, move forward with action. Take a step, no matter how small, and eventually you will succeed.

18. **Remember joy, love, and contentment**. Seek great things, but always come back to what makes you and others happy and fulfilled.

Final Parting Thoughts

One last time, envision your future self:

Who do you want to be? What do you want to have done? What accomplishments will make your life worthy in your own eyes?

It's not about being successful by the metrics of others; it's about championing the life you want to live. Fifty years from now it will be too late to right the ship and start fresh. You won't be able to do the work you need to do. Time won't allow it.

But today marks the Catalyst for your incredible growth. No matter your circumstance, I urge you to join me. I'm inviting you to Bronco's party, I just hope you find your puzzle piece so you can get in.

As long as I'm here on this Earth and breathing, I'll be doing my absolute best to live out my purpose. I hope you decide to do the same, mistakes and all, and live your best life.

To your growth, development, and undying relentlessness to forge ahead,

—Jordan

THANKS FOR READING, FRIEND

Thanks so much for reading and making it to the end. Wow, that's impressive!

If you want more, don't forget to sign up for the free companion course for this book:

https://www.jmring.com/cyd-book/

Enjoy, and don't be afraid to reach out to me at Jordan@jmring.com with any questions or for a motivation boost if you get stuck. I'm happy to help!

OTHER BOOKS BY JORDAN

Go here to browse and purchase other works by Jordan: https://www.jmring.com/jordans-books/

1. Volcanic Momentum: Get Things Done by Setting Destiny Goals, Mastering the Energy Code, and Never Losing Steam
2. The Balance Point: Master the Work-Life Balance, Love What You do, and Become an Unstoppable Entrepreneur

ABOUT THE AUTHOR

Jordan Ring might seem like an intergalactic task-ninja, but he's an authorpreneur at heart. As good as he is with words, his primary goal is to help people live a life of less talk and more action. When he isn't busy creating epic content, Jordan enjoys brainstorming on Trello boards, watching Marvel movies, playing strategy games, drinking coffee, and hanging out with his amazing wife, Miranda. You can see what he's up to on his site at www.jmring.com.

BONUS RESOURCES TO CATALYZE YOUR DESTINY

*Kindle readers: Feel free to use this section for mental exercises or download the printables, enhanced images, and other resources at https://www.jmring.com/cyd-book/

BONUS #1: PERSONAL IDENTITY BLUEPRINT

1) Ask Five Friends One Question

Reach out to five of your closest friends and say something like:

This is random, but a book I'm reading prompted me to ask this of a friend: What do you see as my personal strengths? What is a trait or characteristic unique to me? All feedback is welcome. Thank you. Appreciate your time.

Record their answers here:

1)

2)

3)

4)

5)

2) Take the MBTI Personality Test

Take the MBTI test here for free: https://www.16personalities.com/

Record your type, along with three of the most notable facets of your personality:

Type:

1)

2)

3)

3) CliftonStrengths

Assessment links:

- Take the test here: https://store.gallup.com
- Free High Five Test: https://high5test.com
- StrengthsFinder 2.0 Book: https://store.gallup.com
- Living Your Strengths Book: https://store.gallup.com

Record your top five signature themes below:

1)

2)

3)

4)

5)

What patterns do you see here?

How do you plan to use your strengths moving forward?

4) The Enneagram Personality Test

Take the Enneagram test here:
https://www.truity.com/test/enneagram-personality-test

Record your type and three takeaways below:

Type:

1)

2)

3)

5) Work History Test

Record your answers for the work history test for your three most relevant jobs:

Job 1 Title:

What did you do?

When did you do it?

What three things did you enjoy about it?

1)

2)

3)

What three things did you not enjoy about it?

1)

2)

3)

What is your favorite memory?

Assign an Overall Grade (A-E or 1-10):

Job 2 Title:

What did you do?

When did you do it?

What three things did you enjoy about it?

1)

2)

3)

What three things did you not enjoy about it?

1)

2)

3)

What is your favorite memory?

Assign an Overall Grade (A-E or 1-10):

Job 3 Title:

What did you do?

When did you do it?

What three things did you enjoy about it?

1)

2)

3)

What three things did you not enjoy about it?

1)

2)

3)

What is your favorite memory?

Assign an Overall Grade (A-E or 1-10):

6) Determine Your Core Values

Complete the core values exercises below:

Describe your thoughts and experiences for the following five scenarios:

Picture the most vivid or exciting memory you have of your adult life. What thoughts or feelings do you have?

Picture the last time you got into a heated discussion or debate. Why were you so riled up?

What is your strongest habit? Why?

Picture your perfect day. What kinds of things do you want to experience?

Lastly (and forgive the morbidity), what do you want them to say at your funeral? How would you end this sentence: (Your name) always lived with passion for _____

Using the words from above, determine your top five core value words:

1)

2)

3)

4)

5)

OR Pick 5-10 words from this list (https://www.jmring.com/list-of-core-values/) that resonate with you. Don't overthink it, but do pick words you like

1)

2)

3)

4)

5)

6)

7)

8)

9)

10)

7) Complete a Time Audit

Record your answers to the time audit questions below:

1) What took up most of your time today? (look at your calendar if needed)

2) What do you wish you did more of?

3) What did you do that you probably didn't need to do?

4) What's one thing you can do better tomorrow?

Fill out the table below for a look at your *Ideal* daily schedule (modify as needed):

Time	Activity

8) Refresh Your Life Goals

Record your fifty life goals here:

What are ten things I would like to accomplish? (Examples: Write twenty-five books, sell a business for $10 million, compete in a hot-pepper-eating challenge and win)

1)

2)

3)

4)

5)

6)

7)

8)

9)

10)

What are ten things I would like to see (before…)? (Examples: The Pyramids, my daughter's wedding, the ocean from my screened-in porch.)

1)

2)

3)

4)

5)

6)

7)

8)

9)

10)

What are ten things I would like to become? (Examples: An international speaker, a winner of the Nobel Peace Prize, a screenwriter for Disney/Pixar)

1)

2)

3)

4)

5)

6)

7)

8)

9)

10)

What are ten new things I could try? (Examples: Travel to outer space, cliff dive in Bermuda, win a poker tournament and qualify for the World Series of Poker)

1)

2)

3)

4)

5)

6)

7)

8)

9)

10)

What are ten things I would like to *share* with the world? (Examples: I want my children to share my love for reading, I want to start a successful non-profit, I want to direct an indie film exposing human trafficking that gets picked up by Netflix.)

1)

2)

3)

4)

5)

6)

7)

8)

9)

10)

List the FIVE most important RIGHT-NOW goals from the previous list of 50:

1)

2)

3)

4)

5)

9) The Two-Word Test

Record your two-word exercise here:

Signature Scripture or Favorite Quote:

My strong abilities include:

1)
2)
3)
4)
5)

I have a deep passion for:

1)
2)
3)
4)
5)

I can use these abilities and passion in the context of:

1)
2)
3)
4)
5)

Two-Word Ideas:

1)
2)
3)

10) List Ten Things You Love About Yourself

Quickly list ten of your favorite things about yourself here:

1)

2)

3)

4)

5)

6)

7)

8)

9)

10)

BONUS #2: IKIGAI WORKSHEET

The Ikigai and the Four Points of Purpose

A Japanese Approach to Discovering Life Purpose

Feeling of uselessness. Work doesn't matter.

Lacking financial security. Unsustainable contentment.

What You **Love**

Happy and Productive

Happy and Influential

What You Are **Good** At

Ikigai!

What the World **Needs**

Financial Security and Productive

Influential and Financial Security

Comfortable with status quo. Not passionate about work.

What You Can Get **Paid** For

Lacking skills. Confusion at progress and narrowing of options.

Ikigai Point #1: What Do You Love?

Ikigai Point #2: What Does the World Need?

Ikigai Point #3: What Are You Good At?

Ikigai Point #4: What Can You Get Paid For?

Ikigai Crossover Questions

What you love + what the world needs:

What you love + what you can get paid for:

What you love + what you are good at:

What the world needs + what you can get paid for:

What the world needs + what you are good at:

What you are good at + what you can get paid for:

Ikigai Wrap Up: What Action Ideas Spring to Mind?

BONUS #3: 90-DAY ACTION PLAN TEMPLATE

Name:

Date Range (90 Days):

Goal:

Purpose:

Task List:

Habits to Continue:

Resources Needed:

Notes:

Week One Review Notes:

Week Two Review Notes:

Week Three Review Notes:

Week Four Review Notes:

Week Five Review Notes:

Week Six Review Notes:

Week Seven Review Notes:

Week Eight Review Notes:

Week Nine Review Notes:

Week Ten Review Notes:

Week Eleven Review Notes:

Week Twelve Review Notes:

BONUS EXERCISE: MEASURING PROGRESS. HOW FAR HAVE I COME AND HOW FAR DO I HAVE YET TO GO?

Too often, the weight of anxiety takes over and permeates my life. I let life get to me. But I have a major advantage. I know it's there and ever-present. So I attack it. The habits I form, the decisions I make, and the life I lead need to account for the anxiety that threatens to bring it all down.

I'm not perfect, but self-discovery led to uncovering strengths and understanding the pitfalls I need to watch out for. What are your pitfalls? What has the potential to bring about your downfall? What do you need to work on?

Browse this list and check off the items you feel good about. Don't spend too long on each one. There's no score, and you don't have to turn this in to be graded. This is for you to learn which specific growth areas are important to you. You will never be perfect, but it's important to get better each day.

- ❏ I practice active listening regularly.
- ❏ I know what pitfalls I'm likely to face.
- ❏ I don't make excuses for my actions. Instead, I admit when I'm wrong.
- ❏ I stick up for what's right.
- ❏ I regularly allow myself to breathe deep and let go of deeply held emotions.

- ❑ I can get on my soapboxes, but I recognize the need for humility.
- ❑ There are people out there who are smarter than I am.
- ❑ I believe I have a unique purpose.
- ❑ I regularly take time for myself to nurture my personal growth.
- ❑ I mentor someone else.
- ❑ I have a mentor.
- ❑ I regularly meet with a group of people who hold each other accountable.
- ❑ If I mess up, I quickly admit my mistake and do my best to fix it.
- ❑ I can quickly prioritize a to-do list and not get overwhelmed.
- ❑ I recognize my biases and do my best to understand others.
- ❑ I have healthy boundaries.
- ❑ I respond, I don't react.
- ❑ I practice empathy and love deeply.
- ❑ I think about others more often than just myself.
- ❑ If I get knocked down, I get right back up.
- ❑ I have a healthy dose of optimism and realism.
- ❑ I am honest and live with integrity at all times.
- ❑ I do the hard work today to reap the benefits tomorrow.
- ❑ I show gratitude to family, friends, and strangers regularly.
- ❑ I take time to think, reflect, and plan my next steps.
- ❑ I don't take myself too seriously; what do I know anyway?
- ❑ I will never finish learning and growing.
- ❑ I listen more than I talk (tough one for extraverts, but still a sign of maturity).
- ❑ I don't get offended easily.
- ❑ I don't blame others for my circumstances. Instead, I have a plan to move forward.
- ❑ I don't keep making the same mistakes.

- ☐ I don't judge others who are different from me. Instead, I seek to understand.
- ☐ I give without expecting anything in return.
- ☐ I'm truly happy for someone who succeeds; I don't experience envy.
- ☐ I love who I am right now, but I want to be better.
- ☐ If I say I'm going to do something, I do it.

Action Step: How did you do?

1. *Which checked boxes surprised you?*
2. *Which unchecked items do you plan to check in the future?*

www.ingramcontent.com/pod-product-compliance
Lightning Source LLC
LaVergne TN
LVHW051544080426
835510LV00020B/2841